CAREER AFTER COVID-19

Fleur Hull

with Kym Kraljevic

First published by Ultimate World Publishing 2020
Copyright © 2020 Fleur Hull

ISBN (print edition): 978-1-922497-40-6
ISBN (e-book): 978-1-922497-41-3

- -

We acknowledge the Traditional Owners of the Country throughout Australia and recognise their continuing connection to land, water and community. We pay our respects to them and their cultures and to Elders past, present and emerging.

Career after COVID was written in Western Australia, on the traditional lands of the Nyoongar Whadjuk people, and in Queensland, on the traditional lands of the Waka people.

DEDICATION

This book is dedicated to the billions of people all around the world negatively affected by the ravages of COVID-19, whether through economic hardship, the loss of someone they love, or the virus' effects on their own physical and mental health.

It is also dedicated to the frontline workers everywhere who have been fighting the virus on behalf of us all.

As COVID-19 continues to impact people around the world, we understand that many are struggling to survive, put food on the table or provide shelter for themselves or their family. We recognise we are in the privileged position of living in a safe environment with our survival needs and obligations under control.

We wrote this book for those who have the relative luxury of pondering their career direction at this time. In no way do we intend to discount the trials of life of those who do not have the opportunity to explore their higher-level needs. As a gesture of support, we will contribute part-proceeds of this book to assist some of the most vulnerable people in our community. We hope that as you read this, you are in a relatively safe place in your life and are ready to make the most of any opportunities that this book might present.

To support those who are struggling with their
mental health, 10% of author royalties
from sales of this book throughout 2020 and 2021
will be donated to Beyond Blue, an Australian charity
promoting positive mental wellbeing.

CONTENTS

v

PART THREE: BEING PART OF THE WORLD OF SELF-EMPLOYMENT

INTRODUCTION

Kym and I lost our jobs on the same day in late March 2020. The next day, we spoke at length on the phone to console each other, commiserate and vent our frustrations. Significantly, once we got all this off our chest, we then moved on to a more positive discussion of what action we would take to make the most of our respective situations. Almost immediately, we decided to reconvene the next day and record our conversations to upload them as a publicly available podcast—and at that moment, the *Career after COVID* podcast was born.

At the very least, we agreed that the process of meeting online each week and detailing our current mindset and actions in light of our circumstances would be a form of therapy. If anyone else out in podcast-land got something positive from our discussions, then we saw that as a bonus.

1

We hold a fundamentally optimistic viewpoint on where this virus and its impacts on humanity will take us as a species. We are interested in human beings' capability to survive, thrive and turn a crisis into an opportunity—for growth, learning, the building of resilience and ultimately, success and contentment. Kym and I have also witnessed first-hand the transformative effects of this pandemic, in terms of ways of working, the connections between humans and our sense of ourselves. We sincerely hope that from this, good things will eventually emerge across the world in a range of human endeavours.

For those of you who have picked up this book to find a new way forward, we recognise and validate your struggle. The world of unemployment or career insecurity is an uncomfortable space to exist in, and many of us are currently feeling that discomfort for the first time in our lives.

During our working lives, Kym and I have been through countless CVs, hired hundreds of staff and advised thousands of professionals and students on career direction and growth. We want to share the insight and knowledge we have gained through our experience, highlighting options and providing inspiration to anyone unemployed, underemployed or seeking a significant change as a result of the COVID-19 pandemic. Our podcast audience is gradually building, and we are grateful for their support and feedback. It has provided us with the encouragement needed to write this book as a resource to help others navigate these difficult and challenging times.

Why you need this book

The world of work was already in a state of change before COVID came along. New developments in technology such as automation and casualisation meant that many businesses had already shifted to contracting employees, outsourcing and offshoring many of their tasks. This pattern has led to the emergence of the 'gig economy', where workers can end up having multiple small, part-time contract jobs rather than one full-time job for life.

The mass unemployment created by COVID-19 has resulted in even greater competition for jobs, and whole sectors (such as tourism and aviation) have been virtually wiped out in many parts of the world. Working from home and practising social distancing in the workplace has also changed the way that organisations function, impacting the technology required to undertake all aspects of running a business in today's economy.

It has also shifted the mindset of both employers and employees concerning remote working. Business owners and organisational leaders across the world have been pleasantly surprised by the levels of workforce productivity that has emerged from their employees working from home.

The insecurity of many businesses, however, and the corresponding changes in approach to hiring staff, has meant that everyone has to be aware of the new rules of being and staying employed after the coronavirus. Many of us have experienced a shift in values as a result of working from home—for example, avoiding spending hours each week commuting to and from work and spending more time around our families. For many, the desire to find a more flexible working environment and enjoy a better balance between the things we value has grown more potent as a result.

On top of this, many brick-and-mortar stores have had to close during the pandemic. Most countries have witnessed a steep rise in online shopping and more employment opportunities in the retail sector.

Without an understanding of how the workplace has changed, you may be unemployed or underemployed for longer than expected. You could miss out on the opportunities that the new ways of working are opening up for so many people across the economy.

In this book, we provide you with the information you need to shape your thinking about who you are as a person, uncover your purpose in life and find out which career opportunities match your skills and strengths. We'll also offer some advice on keeping a positive mindset, so you are ready to take advantage of opportunities as they present, and live the professional and personal life you have always wanted.

However, this book goes beyond the simple transfer of information. The actual value lies in the practical advice that guides and supports you as you take the steps that lead you to where you want (and need) to be.

While it's true that the internet is awash with tips, tricks, hacks and ideas that, frankly, you can access instantly, the point of difference in reading this book is that it focuses on **what you can do now** to forge a new and meaningful path in life. The background, research and stories from our own lives that we share are designed to anchor the suggestions for action and help motivate you to make the necessary changes.

5

In many ways, there has never been a better time to reassess our place in the world. The chaos and uncertainty of the pandemic bring with them significant freedoms for many of us. It seems that life has slowed down, and there is a greater level of tolerance of failure and a sense of kindness towards our fellow man that we never had time to exhibit in our hectic, pre-pandemic lives.

We both gain great satisfaction from seeing individuals and organisations reach their true potential. Our wish is for you to emerge from your reading of this book with a clearer sense of who you are, the gifts you have to offer the world of work, and the value you can create for yourself and your family as a result of your career.

How to use this book

Career after COVID is structured to be read and utilised as a guide for the many scenarios that people of working age have found themselves in during the pandemic. It's a useful reference whether you're entirely unemployed, underemployed (either operating fewer hours that you would like to, or working in a role that doesn't fully extend and challenge you), or fully employed but seeking a change in terms of position, industry, working conditions or lifestyle.

We write with the Australian market in mind but have tried to make our advice as relevant to international contexts as possible.

At its heart, this book provides practical, actionable advice that will help you build your ideal career during and after COVID. The value comes from the knowledge we've gained through our career journeys and how that may help you, the reader, to find a fulfilling pathway.

Each chapter ends with a list of tools for action so that you can apply what you've learned productively. The tools provide an action list to refer to later. The rapid evolution of the pandemic and its effects have led us to offer

6

additional information and downloads for free, and without a subscription, from our website.

For ease of use, we have structured the book into three parts. Part One guides your understanding of who you are, what you value in life, how COVID is affecting you and what it means for your current employment status and future career prospects. The aim by the end of these chapters is to clearly understand the reality of your situation, what your goals are, and have a good idea of the type of career options that might suit you.

The second part of the book focuses on your journey back to paid employment, with timely advice on job seeking during COVID and the subsequent recession. Upgrading your skills and knowledge can give your confidence and resume a much-needed boost. Chapter Five provides an overview of education and professional development options available, many of which are now more accessible due to the switch to online learning during the pandemic.

Given the mass levels of unemployment are likely to persist for many months (if not years) in Part Three, we explore self-employment as an option. We outline the entrepreneurial process from idea generation and business model decisions, to planning, launching and growing a business to help you decide if it is something you should do.

Whichever path ends up being right for you, we hope the advice within assists you to make 2021 a successful one for you So, let's get started!

PART ONE

BEING THE MOST EMPLOYABLE YOU

CHAPTER ONE

BECOMING BULLETPROOF

> Your time is limited, so don't waste it living someone else's life. Don't be trapped by dogma—which is living with the results of other people's thinking. Don't let the noise of others' opinions drown out your inner voice. And most important, have the courage to follow your heart and intuition. They somehow already know what you truly want to become. Everything else is secondary.
>
> **STEVE JOBS**

11

Before we get started, a reminder that this book does not provide professional mental health advice. Please seek support and assistance from a medical practitioner or a mental health professional if you're experiencing significant, long-term difficulties with your mood and mindset.

Unemployment descended on us quicker than we imagined. In late March 2020, the Australian Prime Minister's Friday morning exhortations to get on with life as usual and attend the football on the weekend turned to mass lockdowns and shutdowns by Monday morning. Kym and I were both called into our respective employers' boardrooms, and by the end of that Monday, we were packing up our desks.

On Tuesday morning, I dropped my children at school and then dialled Kym, to tell her my news and hear some words of support. Unbeknownst to me, Kym had already begun preparations to move from Sydney back to her home in rural Queensland following her own job loss. As you can imagine, the phone call was taken up with feelings of sadness, and of course, the frustrations and worries of an uncertain future.

We are both spontaneous—some would say 'impulsive' types. The idea to discuss our situation using the public broadcast of a podcast seemed like an excellent way to turn our professional tragedies into something … well, into *anything* that might make a difference.

Along the way, we had doubts and fears about the journey. One of the most challenging feelings to overcome was the sense that we were not qualified to broadcast our stories; what is known as 'imposter syndrome'. We supported each other through these feelings and became, in many ways, accountability coaches, ensuring we stayed on track with our self-development, as well as our job search progress.

As we've continued my research for this book, we have reflected on our journey and in particular, which of the scientifically-validated mindset tools and success factors we've instinctively deployed along the way. Some of these are outlined here as part of our story.

Why a healthy mindset is essential right now

As a result of the pandemic, you may be unemployed, underemployed or just seeking a change, but you know that your current state cannot continue indefinitely. That's why you've picked up this book. We've all grieved and are still grieving for the personal life we used to lead. Depending upon where you are in the world, you may have lost your ability to regularly travel outside of your house entirely or have your options for interaction with others severely limited.

A survey of 13,829 Australian adults conducted in April 2020 found that mental health problems were at least twice as prevalent than they had been in non-pandemic circumstances[1]. More than ever, our resilience and emotional strength are being tested and, in many ways, our ability to cope and thrive in this time will define our lives for the foreseeable future.

---

[1] Fisher, JRW, Tran, TD, Hammarberg, K, Sastry, J, Nguyen, H, Rowe, H, Popplestone, S, Stocker, R, Stubber, C, Kirkman, M 2020, 'Mental health of people in Australia in the first month of COVID-19 restrictions: a national survey. *Medical Journal of Australia*, published online, 10 June 2020: https://www.mja.com.au/journal/2020/mental-health-people-australia-first-month-covid-19-restrictions-national-survey

What is 'mindset'?

You can describe your mindset as the way you approach your life, guided by your opinions and way of thinking. Some examples of different types of mindset include a positive outlook, optimistic view of life, an abundance mindset, an entrepreneurial mindset or a businessperson's investment mindset. As with many facets of our humanity, various researchers and writers have formulated definitions and so-called 'definitive lists' of mindset types.

According to Stanford University Psychology Professor Carol Dweck in her book, *Mindset: The New Psychology of Success*, there are two types of mindsets: a fixed mindset and a growth mindset. People with a fixed mindset believe fundamental qualities, like intelligence or talent, are simply fixed traits and that talent alone creates success—without effort. Those with a growth mindset believe that the most basic abilities can be developed through dedication and hard work. It is the latter, growth mindset view, which creates resilience and a love of learning.[2]

Resilience is the ability to adjust when faced with adversity positively, and such a mindset is critical in a time of crisis like this. We are all born with a baseline biological level of determination and resilience, and those with high levels of

---

[2]   Dweck, CS 2006, *Mindset: the new psychology of success*, Random House, New York.

emotional intelligence are likely to be predisposed with an ability to cope well and thrive in difficult times[3].

This chapter will provide you with our most practical tips for shaping your mindset positively, based on the latest research that occurred before, and importantly, during, the pandemic. We also share the insights we've gathered from our own experience of unemployment and uncertainty, our podcast episodes, and one-on-one consulting work with clients.

More than anything, our life and career experiences have shown us that many of our breakthrough moments or significant successes have come along after a period marked by fear, crisis or self-doubt. The clichés can ring true in these circumstances: when one door closes another one opens, everything happens for a reason and so on. COVID-19 is already revealing some unexpectedly positive outcomes, including the kindness of humanity in times of crisis and this chapter will help you to see the potential for your mindset to allow you to capitalise on those opportunities.

---

[3] Rimfeld, K, Kovas, Y, Dale, PS, & Plomin, R 2016 'True grit and genetics: Predicting academic achievement from personality', *Journal of Personality and Social Psychology*, 111(5), 780-789. http://dx.doi.org/10.1037/pspp0000089

How to enhance your mindset and build resilience

Getting real

One of the seminal books in my professional education has been *Good to Great* by Jim Collins. His epic research project of thousands of businesses resulted in the distillation of critical factors that he posits will lead to sustained commercial success. In particular, the examples outlined in Chapter four, titled, 'Confront the Brutal Facts (Yet Never Lose Faith)' have always reminded me to accept the brutal reality of my circumstances, however painful they are, and to not be in denial about what has occurred.[4]

Another technique I have learned and utilised over the years includes giving myself the space to adjust to changes. I practise being kind to myself, sitting with the discomfort of my current reality without judgement of my role in, or blame for, my circumstances. During COVID, this has been an incredibly helpful technique. Like so many other unemployed people, the conditions that led to my job loss were entirely out of my hands.

Marking transitions

To improve my mindset and prepare for opportunities, I have allowed myself to grieve and recognise the personal

16

---

[4] Collins, JC 2001, *Good to great: why some companies make the leap . . . and others don't*, Harper Business. New York.

and professional costs of the pandemic. I've taken the time to feel the sense of loss and to mark the transitions between my pre-pandemic existence and my current reality. It has become a useful form of mindfulness.

Throughout my adult life, I have found that making a ritual out of these transitions, including celebrating when I achieve quick wins along the way, has assisted me to move to the point of acceptance of my circumstances. These rituals allow me to progress without dwelling on the losses.

Forgiveness

Forgiveness is an integral part of this, especially self-forgiveness and letting go of the inclination to blame ourselves for what has occurred. While blaming others can seem like a comforting way to externalise the causes of our problems, in the longer term it is not helpful, as it delays the process of moving on. Thoughts of revenge or retribution aimed at those we feel have wronged us are very human reactions and completely understandable in a time of stress. Ultimately, however, they erode our chance to chart a positive path to success on our own terms. I always remind myself of my mother's signature piece of advice when these negative thoughts creep into my mind: *"Retain your dignity."*

Finding purpose

Numerous studies, including one in the *Journal of Aging and Mental Health*, have confirmed the links between levels of resilience and living a life of purpose.[5] 'Purpose in life predicts both health and longevity, suggesting that the ability to find meaning from life's experiences, especially when confronting life's challenges, may be a mechanism underlying human resilience.'[6]

We explore this concept further in Chapter Three: Do what you love, love what you do.

Gratitude

Throughout our podcasting journey, Kym and I have absorbed a great deal of information, while also reflecting on our own lives this far. One tip that emerged from our reading was the concept of gratitude as a way to increase positive thoughts. Appreciation for what I have is a tool that I used to employ during my busy full-time working life before my children were born, but it had lapsed at some point along the way. I have coached myself to replace guilt and shame with gratitude, and as soon as I brought it back into my conscious daily practice, I noticed an immediate lift in my perception of my circumstances.

18

---

[5] Nygren, B, Aléx, L, Jonsén, E, Gustafson, Y, Norberg, A & Lundman, B 2005, 'Resilience, sense of coherence, purpose in life and self-transcendence in relation to perceived physical and mental health among the oldest old', *Aging & Mental Health*, vol 9(4), pp. 354–62, DOI: 10.1080/1360500114415

[6] Schaefer, SM, Morozink, BJ, van Reekum, CM, Lapate, RC, Norris, CJ, Ryff, CD & Davidson, RJ 2013, 'Purpose in life predicts better emotional recovery from negative stimuli', *PLOS One*, vol. 8(11):e80329. Published 2013 Nov 13. doi:10.1371/journal.pone.0080329

Many mindset and mental health professionals recommend specific activities like keeping a gratitude journal as a vital way to formalise this positive thinking each day.

Facing fears

Kym and I regularly explored our fears on the podcast, to try and understand the thoughts and attitudes that may be holding us back from where we want to be. If you're experiencing feelings of fear, investigate them deeply and challenge them. Understand what is keeping you from getting started with your job or business ideas and being the best version of yourself in this time of difficulty.

Some of the most common fears and reasons for not taking action include:

- fear of failure, rejection or ridicule
- fear of disappointing or letting others down
- not knowing how to get started, or what the process is to move your ideas forward
- fear of choosing the wrong job or business idea
- fear of not being qualified or knowledgeable enough
- fear that your idea isn't original or if it is, that others may copy it
- a very pertinent fear in times of COVID: you're worried that you don't have the money or the time to get started, because you're focused on just surviving and making ends meet

- fear of success—the worry that you won't be able to cope if the idea you have takes off and becomes something big and real.

Explore each of these types of fear and think of ways to overcome or work around it. One of my favourite techniques is to imagine the worst-case scenario if I take a particular course of action. Knowing the worst that can happen (and usually working out how remote a possibility it is), often helps me to see I have more to gain than to lose.

Remember, so many people are feeling fear and additional discomfort at this time, and they're more likely to welcome your activities and outreach without a feeling of judgement towards you.

Imposter syndrome

Related to our fears, is the concept of the imposter syndrome. It is the psychological phenomenon first described by psychologists Suzanne Imes and Pauline Rose Clance in the 1970s[7]. It often occurs among high achievers who are unable to internalise and accept their success. They attribute their accomplishments to luck rather than to ability or hard work and fear that others will eventually discover them as a fraud or imposter. These feelings and thoughts are highlighted for

---

[7] Clance, PR & Imes, SA 1978, The imposter phenomenon in high achieving women: Dynamics and therapeutic intervention, *Psychotherapy: Theory, Research & Practice*, vol 15(3), pp. 241-47. https://doi.org/10.1037/h0086006

those whose employment has become precarious because of COVID. The loss of a job feels like a confirmation of their self-doubt.

Although it is not described as a mental health disorder, seeking help from a mental health professional can be beneficial for those suffering from what can be a debilitating mindset. Rewriting your internal dialogue is a difficult task to accomplish without support.

Mentors and support networks

When faced with upheaval, it's natural to first think of 'what to do?' and 'how to do it?'. As natural extroverts who get energy from our interactions with others, Kym and I added 'who can help me?' to our list of questions. We knew we could be a support for each other, as well as brainstorming who else might be able to assist. Our networks and community of supporters are so important at a time of crisis.

The challenge during COVID-19 is that everyone is undergoing upheaval and crisis simultaneously. Not everyone that we might usually rely on for support is capable of devoting energy while dealing with their own struggles. We have both found this to be a delicate balancing act in our interactions. On the one hand, the pandemic has brought out the best in so many people. Understandably, there has been negativity to cope with as well. Providing support for those we care about is important to us, and we have done our utmost to be a listening ear or a socially-distanced virtual hug for those in need.

In a less beneficial sense, there are always going to be people whose instinct is one of negativity and victimhood. Given our own challenges, from time to time, we have had to excuse ourselves politely from situations where we've been getting dragged down by other people's less-than-positive thoughts. We have also made a very conscious choice to avoid comparing ourselves with others. We are focused on running our own race according to our individual values and goals.

Self-care

The basics of self-care are more important than ever these days, but not always easy to implement. Sleepless nights worrying about finances and comfort eating when things get stressful have been common along the way. Focus on your own self-care and your physical and mental health first. Exercising regularly, eating healthily and taking regular breaks apply more than ever in this time of transition.

Another great tip is to focus on following a morning routine, to get your day underway with positivity. Kym and I have encouraged each other to start the day **without** first touching our phones. We have, instead, been taking a moment to be mindful of the opportunities that the day provides after we wake up. After I wake up, I consciously sit up in bed and just smile. It's remarkable how much a smile improves my sense of optimism before I get on my phone for the day and discover the bad COVID news or the number of tasks that I have to undertake.

Optimism and humour

I have been fortunate to have grown up in a household that valued playfulness and humour as a way to cope with adversity. One of my mother's favourite sayings is, 'If you don't laugh, you'll end up crying'. Without it becoming too much of a bad habit, I have allowed myself regular humour breaks throughout these challenging months. These occasions have included watching my favourite comedy on television or scrolling through comedians' posts on social media (shout-out to Sarah Cooper, whose uncanny impressions have made my day on so many occasions). It's okay to see the funny side of things, even in the darkest of moments.

Pitfalls to avoid

As the months of living with the coronavirus stretch on, it is inevitable that we feel a sense of fatigue at the constant COVID news updates, the restrictions on our lives and the challenge of isolation and disconnection from our pre-pandemic way of being.

The spiral downwards into feelings of hopelessness and malaise can be sudden and can make us want to retreat

23

and isolate even more. A helpful technique that Kym and I have deployed is making a conscious effort to connect in meaningful ways with our inner circle. Avoiding the trap of withdrawal and instead pushing ourselves to relate (especially over a video link where we can observe the humanity of others) has been the most effective approach we have found to stay in good mental health.

The other pitfall we have worked hard to avoid is a false growth mindset. This is the belief that we are welcoming the challenge of learning and growing, but are actually relatively rigid in our thinking. For me, the onset of the pandemic caused an almost obsessive-compulsive focus on daily case statistics around the world as a way to feel in control of a very chaotic situation. What I didn't realise at the time was that my focus on the data was preventing me from shaping my existence within this new reality.

Summary

COVID has brought significant changes to the way we live and interact with others. The techniques outlined in this chapter are a snapshot of some of the ways to refocus your mind and adapt to these changes. Through the early months of the pandemic, Kym and I worked through each of these approaches, some consciously, some intuitively. We believe these techniques have provided us with some of the sense of calm and optimism required to move forward with our professional and personal goals.

Humans are social creatures, and we cannot stress enough the importance of regularly connecting with fellow human beings in whichever ways you're permitted and able to. We know we're playing the long game with this virus, and our success in reducing its negative impacts is contingent on our working together and supporting our fellow humans.

Tools for action

1) Find and deploy ways to keep your thinking in this current moment. There are many mindfulness tools available to assist with staying present in your environment, including apps such as Smiling Mind.

2) Observe the ways you communicate your identity or approach to life. Our identity shapes our self-belief, our habits and the way others see us too. Instead of 'I'm unemployed', think of positive (but authentic) reframes such as 'I'm planning my next career move' or 'I'm working on my skills and education to prepare for future

opportunities'. Frame your goals in the present rather than the future. For example, instead of saying 'I'm trying to lose more weight', say 'I'm a health-conscious person". Self-talk and affirmations can also be helpful in re-framing your attitudes and mindset.

3) A simple exercise that my authoring mentor taught me is to ask yourself the following questions:
   a. What is something that you have wanted to do but haven't done yet?
   b. What was the lie you told yourself that has slowed you down or stopped you?
   c. What is one small step you can take now to break free from the lie and go after the thing you want to do?
   d. What is the worst thing that can happen if you go after what you truly want?

As with all the chapters in this book, we've produced supplementary material that you can access for free, without the requirement of an email subscription, from our website. This material is updated regularly to consider new research and developments.

Please see https://www.careeraftercovid.com/ mindset for a list of available resources.

CHAPTER TWO

WHO IS IN THE MIRROR?

- -

Knowing yourself is the beginning of all wisdom.

ARISTOTLE

Not until we are lost do we begin to understand ourselves.

HENRY DAVID THOREAU

Throughout history, every external change of the magnitude of COVID-19 has forced human beings to re-evaluate who and where we are, and what is important to us. There are myriad ways to find more out about who you are, and even the smallest insight you gain from this process could provide the seed of a new career direction or business idea.

When COVID-19 left us both unemployed, Kym and I separately sought out the validation and direction that self-analysis provides, undertaking several questionnaires to gain some external confirmation of our true selves after such an upheaval.

We took the time to get to know who was looking at us when we peered into the mirror. So often in the busy-ness of life, we can lose sight of what motivates us and helps us cope—our personality and our unique combination of traits, feelings, attitudes and attributes.

There are many tools available to get to know yourself, the way nature and nurture has shaped you and which life direction or directions suit you. In this chapter, we will provide a brief overview of the ways to 'discover' yourself, as well as many references to tools to continue the journey of self-understanding.

Apart from these tools and tests, the most powerful exercise I undertook was a session with Kym, where we worked out what my professional 'unfair advantage' was:

What is it about me that sets me apart from all the other job applicants or entrepreneurs, and how can I leverage and communicate that to reach my goals?

We'll explore that question in more detail in this chapter along with the other methods we have used along the way of self-discovery.

Why is self-understanding necessary?

From a career perspective, understanding your strengths and weaknesses enables you to present yourself to potential employers in the most compelling way. At its most elementary and fundamental level, the employment relationship is a sales transaction: the candidate is 'selling' their services and the employer is 'purchasing' these services in the belief that the employee will assist in reaching the business' goals.

When applying and interviewing for a job, the self-awareness that comes from knowing your strengths and weaknesses assists you in communicating your value to the potential employer. Besides, having a clear sense of which jobs and types of roles you are suited to demonstrates to a potential employer that you are more likely to be satisfied working in that role, because you've already thought deeply about its suitability.

From a purely personal perspective, profile tests and personality indicators can help to validate what you know about yourself and help you to feel 'understood' and 'seen' in these uncertain times. They can give you a sense of agency when you're in a time of transition. Once you've 'met' yourself using one of these tests, you can assess whether your strengths and preferences indicate a likelihood of achieving your goals. In this way, the results will assist you in planning and taking action to reach these goals.

The other aspect of self-assessment that many people find useful is gaining a greater understanding of personal values. Assessing your value system during the pandemic reminds you of your purpose for being, which will help you to identify if you are working towards the things that truly matter to you.

According to organisational psychologist and author Tasha Eurich, the vast majority of people—up to 95%, in fact—believe they have a decent amount of self-awareness. But according to her research, 'On a good day, 80% of us are lying to ourselves about whether we're lying to ourselves'.[8]

As someone who likes to think of herself as self-aware, these statistics shocked me. Having made career mistakes and life choices in the past based on an incorrect or biased view of myself, I thought I'd learned from those misjudgements through many years of self-reflection and development.

Two periods in my life stand out when I think about missteps due to lack of self-awareness. The first is a relatively common one—my choice of university majors after I finished school. After a gap year living in Japan, I enrolled in a Bachelor of Computer and Mathematical Sciences. I made this choice partly because I'd enjoyed those subjects at school, but mainly because labour market economists

[8] Eurich, T 2017, *Insight: The surprising truth about how others see us, how we see ourselves, and why the answers matter more than we think*, Currency, New York.

predicted that there would be thirteen jobs available for every graduate of courses like that (which is no doubt still valid). What I didn't realise was that my personality traits (especially my extroversion) were not suited to a course which mainly involved solitary work at a computer. In the end, I 'wasted' a semester of university and the subject fees. However, the self-knowledge (and the knowledge that I needed self-knowledge!) was a significant gain through the process.

The other episode involved my early years as a manager, which coincided with my postgraduate studies in management. I was fortunate to undertake the Myers-Briggs Type Indicator (MBTI) test as part of a unit of study called, 'Managing Change', taught by a remarkable organisational psychologist named Dr Ann Zubrick. The subject matter enabled each of the students to reflect on their assigned type and preferences generally, but also within the context of organisational change.

There isn't space in a book of this type to go into minute detail on the workings of the MBTI (the 16personalities.com website is my favourite reference source). In the context of my career episode, I learned that I had a preference for 'thinking' (organising and structuring information to make decisions in a logical, objective way). Conversely, the eight people reporting to me, as well as my boss, appeared to have preferences for 'feeling' (organising and structuring information to make decisions in a personal, values-oriented way), which was a profound revelation. This knowledge significantly enhanced my management abilities, especially in times of organisational transition.

How to gain a better understanding of who you are

Humans are often drawn to tools to understand who we are during times of transition or stress. When life is sailing along peacefully, we are unlikely to spend the time reflecting on what's working in our lives or how we can move forward beyond the trajectory we are on. In the days following being made redundant from my very-new job in March 2020, I found my *Introduction to Type* book that was one of my texts for the aforementioned postgraduate change management subject in 2001[9].

I retook the test and received a slightly different combination of preferences from those I had received nineteen years earlier. It encouraged in me the desire to explore my traits and preferences further, especially in the context of change. I asked myself several questions:

- How have I changed over the years of my working life, and how has the pandemic changed me specifically?

---

[9] Hirsch, S & Kummerow, J 1998, *Introduction to type in organisations*, Consulting Psychology Press, California.

- Do the updated results for my personality traits and preferences ring true?
- How do I feel about the changes in me as a person, as well as any externally driven changes?
- Do I feel the drive to change in other ways to adapt to the pandemic?
- What are my intrinsically driven values?
- What are the external rewards that drive and motivate me?
- Do my daily habits and behaviours align with my values and motivations?

Personality indicators fall into one of two main categories: projective and objective. The Rorschach test is an example of a projective test. These types of tests are based on the assumption that personality is an unconscious construct, so they ask subjects to project meaning onto an image, and experts interpret the implications according to validated norms.

Objective tools and tests such as the Enneagram, The Personality Self-Portrait, The Big Five, the Myers-Briggs Type Indicator and DISC Personality Profile provide a score that distinguishes the characteristics of an individual in relation to others.

We provide an overview of all of the validated personality and values tests in the 'Tools for Action' references at the end of this chapter.

How to find your unfair advantage

If the concept of your unfair advantage is new to you, or if nothing immediately comes to mind, the most direct way to find out what your superpower is, is to ask the people that know you the best. Post a question on your personal social media pages or email a dozen of your family members, closest friends and trusted colleagues.

The responses I got from this exercise demonstrated that the people close to me saw me as someone bold, fearless, easy to get along with and engaged with the world around me.

I wanted to go more in-depth on these concepts and think about what truly sets me apart in an employment or business context. Kym was my next stop: Kym's superpower is her ability to hone in on other people's superpowers and unfair advantages! I took the opportunity to avail myself of her skills, and we conversed via video conference to get to the heart of what makes me unique.

I outlined my upbringing in a family that was engaged in several small businesses across diverse industries. I then listed the companies my parents had owned and operated:

- spice distributor
- pasta factory
- three lunch bars and cafes (at different times)

- pickle factory
- two garden centres and landscaping operations (at different times)
- store protection and secret shopping provider
- document binding business
- ergonomic furniture retailer
- retailer of whiteboards and other educational hard goods
- office design and fit-out business.

I then ran through the list of jobs that I had held throughout my career:

- supermarket checkout cashier
- fish and chips shop cashier
- volunteer charity collector
- gift store sales assistant
- Japanese folk dancing parade leader
- surf shop sales assistant
- coordinator for international relations in a Japanese government office
- speechwriter and communications officer for a lord mayor
- university course and career adviser
- university marketing and admissions manager
- search engine optimisation copywriter
- operations and external relations manager for a new university campus

- chief of staff and senior policy advisor to the vice-chancellor and president of a university
- Indian folk-art dealer
- marketing and PR director for a blockchain energy start-up
- T-shirt designer and retailer
- careers coach and candidate marketing professional.

I pondered out loud how these experiences had shaped my understanding of the world of work and the economy in general, as well as my ideal place in it. It quickly became apparent to Kym that my unfair advantage is the wide range of industries and roles I had experienced and observed throughout my life. Although I knew these experiences had built in me a strong business acumen, I had not reflected on the diversity and how that gave me a superpower when it comes to advising others on their life choices. Along the way, we also discussed many of Kym's workplace experiences and could see how our diverse backgrounds had drawn us together as friends and now co-authors. My favourite paid job that Kym had was a role in England where she dressed sheep in leg-warmers!

How to assess which industries and jobs will suit you

Following our job loss and subsequent self-assessment of what makes us who we are, Kym and I moved to an external assessment, and we started assessing our suitability for specific roles and how we fitted into the job market.

We also reflected on the full range of work experiences throughout our lives. We took the opportunity to assess what it was about each of them that we loved and which aspects were not so enjoyable or fulfilling. This process gave us both some excellent insights into our personalities, motivations and working styles. For me, it reinforced my understanding of my preference for extraversion and getting energy from my interactions with others. I remembered the high levels of satisfaction I get from feeling that I have made a difference to an organisation or people, or had some role in their success.

39

We used the acronym 'CLAMPS' as one of our frameworks for what we wanted in our next job. It's a useful career tool that I've been employing in my career advisory consulting for many years, and it's in such common usage I'm not sure who taught it to me all those years ago. CLAMPS is a framework for reflection on the qualities of previous roles and whether they suited our needs and wants.

The letters in CLAMPS stand for:

C – Challenge of the job: Do you need to be presented with regular opportunities for challenge and stimulation?

L – Location: Does the location of your office affect your satisfaction? How does the length of the commute, the neighbourhood of your office (e.g. nice part of town, lots of cafes and shops nearby) contribute to your willingness to stay working in that job compared with other roles? Is there easy access to work from home opportunities, especially in light of COVID?

A – Advancement: Is the opportunity to get more senior experience and move up the ranks of an organisation important to you, or do you shun leadership opportunities?

M – Money/benefits: What proportion of your job satisfaction comes from your base salary? How do other benefits such as bonuses, flexibility or additional superannuation contributions interact with your assessment of remuneration and its importance to your feeling of worth and contentment?

P – People: Are your professional relationships with your colleagues and supervisors important to you, or do you prefer to work alone with limited interaction? How does the quality of your interactions with your co-workers impact on your job satisfaction?

S – Stability and job security: How do you cope with lack of stability and constant change in your work? Are you invigorated by regular changes, or is security and stability critical to your sense of contentment at work?

Kym and I spent time on via video conference discussing the relative levels of importance of each of these elements. We documented them in the worksheet we have provided for your reference on our website, careeraftercovid.com/clamps. We reflected on how COVID had changed the scope of employers' offerings. For example, remote working had taken location out of the equation for many jobs, as had the security of tenure. As a result, these criteria ranked somewhat lower in our assessment of what would drive our job search.

These insights proved to be fundamental in the journey I've taken so far in 2020. The reminders of what motivates and energises me have directed my efforts towards job applications and business ideas that will enable me to stay motivated and satisfied, and away from those that diverge from who I am.

Is running your own business the way forward?

This exact question was one that we explored in Episode seventeen of the *Career after COVID* podcast because so many aspiring entrepreneurs rightly question their suitability for business life before embarking on the journey to business ownership.

In addition to a self-analysis, it can be helpful to look more broadly at the competitive landscape, whether you are looking for work as an employee or starting your own enterprise. Spend some time getting to know who your potential competitors are for the types of roles that you aspire to, through research using tools such as LinkedIn. If you feel comfortable, reach out to these people and form a network of like-minded professionals. You never know when you may need to engage with them in the future, and they could end up as valuable collaborators or supporters down the track.

Pitfalls to avoid

The use of personality tests in employee recruitment processes is well-documented, along with many opinions on their validity and pitfalls as a selection tool. Their widespread use in organisations, however, means that more than a passing familiarity with these tests may assist you while navigating your job-seeking journey.

More importantly, we believe in the benefits that accrue in terms of self-awareness and insight for any individual when they take one or more of these tests. The results are not always 100% scientifically valid, so we advise caution with their interpretation. Suppose you're seeking to make fundamental life changes based on these tests. In that case, it is prudent to consult a certified psychologist that specialises in psychometric testing to provide feedback and validation of your results.

Summary

Self-awareness comes from an understanding of your authentic inner self, as well as a recognition of how you fit in with the external world. Research shows that self-awareness is a crucial ingredient in workplace success. The upheaval brought on by the pandemic has meant that many people facing workplace uncertainty have turned to self-assessment tools to validate who they are and hopefully provide some direction for their future.

Tools for action

1) Undertake one or more personality test or indicators. These include the Enneagram, The Personality Self-Portrait, The Big Five, the Myers-Briggs Type Indicator and DISC Personality Profile. Reflect on the results and how they relate to you both personally and professionally.

2) Put aside some time to identify your skills, interests and talents. Ask yourself, "What excites me?" and think about times in your personal and professional lives when you've felt invincible or unusually strong and adept. Which part of the newspaper do you naturally turn to, or when in a shopping centre, which stores do you like to browse? Ask your friends and family members which skills and talents they observe in you.

3) Undertake a career suitability quiz or skills match, like the quizzes available at joboutlook. gov.au, to see which types of jobs might suit you the best. Review your options with the filter that you want to find a job that will make you excited to get out of bed.

44

The above suggestions are just some of the well-known tools and testing instruments available at the time of writing. We update information regularly and provide links to various testing sites on our website.

You can access the latest resources here: https://www.careeraftercovid.com/tools

CHAPTER THREE

DO WHAT YOU LOVE, LOVE WHAT YOU DO

It doesn't interest me what you do for a living. I want to know what you ache for—and if you dare to dream of meeting your heart's longing. It doesn't interest me how old you are. I want to know if you will risk looking like a fool—for love—for your dreams—for the adventure of being alive.

ORIAH MOUNTAIN DREAMER

47

The COVID pandemic and associated lockdown periods have meant many of us have had time to consider the people and activities that give us the most satisfaction. For some, that thinking has included an analysis of our purpose or mission in our personal and professional lives.

On the *Career after COVID* podcast, Episode 15, we discussed leaving a legacy through your work and career. We asked our listeners to think about what their purpose or mission was in their professional lives. The episode encouraged listeners to reflect on what they wish to be remembered for, as an employee or business owner, and whether they aspired to be involved in a career that's more than just about making a living.

Why consider the purpose or mission of your professional life?

We all know at least one person who appears from the outside as successful and content but who, for some reason, is dissatisfied with where they are in life. Examples we have come across include the partner of a top-tier law firm earning close to a million dollars a year who wishes he could leave that life and go and build houses for poverty-stricken African people. Then there's the medical doctor who felt family pressure to pursue medicine when all she wants to do is play jazz music. There are scores of people in our networks who yearn for what they see as their real calling in life.

Ultimately, many people agree that working in a role that speaks to their soul assists them to feel energised by the bigger purpose that their work is serving. Human beings, as a race, crave a sense of meaning and purpose, and the reflection time that the pandemic has brought upon us all has made this search for meaning even starker.

That's not to say that the quest for wealth and success for its own ends is not a form of value-driven employment.

Valuing material wealth isn't necessarily a harmful objective unless your pursuit of money comes at the expense of other people or the environment. But using "If I had more money..." as an excuse for eschewing the rigorous self-analysis required to assess what **truly** gives you pleasure and satisfaction in life can be a trap. The people that avoid this soul-searching can end up spending their twilight years realising they can't take their fortune with them. They often get to the end of their lives full of regret for the other occupations and pursuits that could've provided them with more meaning and satisfaction.

While on your job search or road to entrepreneurship, you may wish to include an assessment of the alignment of a particular role or organisation with your values and sense of purpose. Some people rule out specific industries or professions because of their belief systems. For example, I could never work for a tobacco company or fossil fuel enterprise, even though they often employee benefits significantly above those for similar roles.

The idea of making a difference is a very strong drawcard for mission-driven organisations. In addition to the benefits of feeling a sense of greater purpose, the smaller scale of many non-profit organisations means that employees often get an opportunity to wear many different hats. The opportunity to undertake a broader range of job tasks and learning opportunities is often hard to experience in a very hierarchical, large corporate organisation. You may get to work more closely with your boss and the leadership team and build a sense of transparency and trust that is trickier to achieve in a large for-profit. The ability to take on more varied tasks with closer involvement with organisational leaders can add skills and experiences to your CV that you wouldn't otherwise have the chance to include.

The smaller size of non-profit organisations also means you will feel like an essential member of the team, rather than just an employee number, and studies show that this can add to your feelings of job satisfaction and enjoyment.

Research from the Bankwest Curtin Economic Centre in 2017 found that a higher proportion of employees in the private sector report being dissatisfied with their job overall (20%) compared to government (14%) and not-for-profit (12%) sector employees.[10]

When I left the higher education sector in 2004 to gain experience in another industry, I worked in an internet marketing and website development company. The work was exciting and the people impressive, but after eleven months I realised I missed the sense of a greater purpose that working in education gave me. Since that time, I have

---

[10] Bankwest Curtin Economics Centre 2018, *Future of Work in Australia*, report, Bankwest Curtin Economics Centre, Perth, viewed 27 August 2020, <https://bcec.edu.au/assets/BCEC-Future-of-Work-in-Australia-Report.pdf.>

only worked in organisations that are delivering more than just financial returns for shareholders. There aren't many more rewarding feelings than seeing the students you had advised and supported into university study graduate at the end of their degrees, with all the promise and excitement of their careers ahead of them!

There is much literature on the regrets that people have as they approach the end of their lives, including a 2019 study by McCrindle Research involving more than 1000 Australians. One of the top responses was the regret that people expressed that they had not contributed more to the greater good. [11]

Moving through life without attention to your values and a sense of purpose could mean that you get to old age with some of the major regrets that others cite. And by then it may be too late to make the contribution you wanted to.

Apart from projecting into the future of your old age, the 'here and now' benefits of working with a purpose are manifold and often accrue to the community at large.

---

11 McCrindle, M 2019, *Aussies' biggest regrets are that they didn't do more with the time they had*, survey report, McCrindle, Sydney, viewed 27 August 2020, <https://mccrindle.com.au/insights/blog/aussies-biggest-life-regrets-are-that-they-didnt-do-more-with-the-time-they-had/.>

What form does a mission-driven career path take?

A large proportion of mission or purpose-driven work takes place in organisations in the not-for-profit sector of the economy, in the following industries:

- education
- the environment
- health and aged care
- religious organisations
- community services—serving marginalised communities such as Indigenous people, domestic violence victims and minority groups.

Also, there are opportunities within the private sector to undertake work with a purpose beyond profit through 'triple bottom line' and corporate social responsibility imperatives. Many medium to large businesses that are traditionally profit-driven have implemented programs or divisions within their structure that support a more significant purpose through the success of the commercial operations.

How to use your values to guide your career

A values assessment can provide you with some insight as to the value you place on contributing to a purpose beyond

52

your own needs. One of the tests I undertook was the Portrait Values Questionnaire, which is based on Schwartz's theory of values. In 2001, Schwartz posited that ten fundamental individual values influence human actions at any point.

These are:

1. **Self-directional values** that define our goals and ambitions in life
2. **Stimulative values** that provide the energy and vigour to move ahead for accomplishing the aspirations
3. **Hedonistic values** that operate on the pleasure principle and instant need for gratification
4. **Achievement values** that define personal success and competence
5. **Power values** that come with societal norms, control and personal resources
6. **Security values** including personal safety, harmony, interpersonal relationships and self-control
7. **Conformity values** that operate through agreeableness to societal norms and standards
8. **Traditional values** involving respect, community support, commitment and acceptance of customs and culture
9. **Benevolent values** which link to the preservation and enhancement of the welfare of self and others close to us

53

10. Universal values that encompass appreciation, tolerance and general acceptance of the nature of things around us.

The ten values in this scale are organised into four domains:

- a self-directional domain that operates on openness and flexibility to change
- a universal value domain that is influenced by transcendence
- a traditional values domain that is motivated by the laws of conservation
- a power value domain that is governed by self-enhancement.[12]

The assessment involves rating each of several statements about how we feel about ourselves and others, according to what we think is most appropriate for us. The results explain which of the four domains play a predominant role in our life and also suggests how to make the most of it.

For me, the top value that most strongly motivates me is number two: universalism. According to this test, this means that I mostly value 'big' goals, exemplified by understanding and tolerance of all people and nature.

---

[12] Schwartz, SH 2012, 'An Overview of the Schwartz Theory of Basic Values', *Online Readings in Psychology and Culture*, vol. 2(1) http://dx.doi.org/10.9707/2307-0919.1116.

The following questions can also provide a helpful framework for your self-assessment:

- What purpose does your life serve?
- What would you do with your time if you had all of your wildest material needs taken care of – say, $20 million in the bank? How would the days and years ahead look different for you if you weren't striving to make ends meet?
- If you run or work in a business, why does this business exist? What does it offer, who does it serve and how does it serve your customers in ways that other firms do not?
- Can I pivot my current working life into something that is mission-based? Think of volunteer opportunities with mission-based organisations you admire or start a social enterprise.

In the podcast, Kym and I discussed one of my favourite books, *The Seven Habits of Highly Effective People* by Stephen R. Covey.[13] Chapter 2 (Habit Two), asks the reader to imagine their eulogy and what might be said by the people close to them. Although it is slightly morbid, it has always reminded me to 'start with the end in mind' and shape my behaviours around helping others.

---

[13] Covey, SR & Collins, JC 2015, *The 7 habits of highly effective people: powerful lessons in personal change*, Brilliance Audio, Michigan.

More than anything, I would like to one day be remembered as a wonderful mother, daughter, sister, friend and community contributor. Although there have been periods of my life where my professional life has strongly shaped my sense of self, I invest the most in my personal relationships. COVID has made this all the more prominent in my thinking, and the values systems of many people throughout the world.

Pitfalls to avoid

Like so many aspects of our lives, acting with integrity and authenticity go a long way to smoothing our path. It's vital to be sure of your motivations for working in a mission-driven role: it will only make sense long term if your drive comes from within, rather than because you feel it is expected of you by others.

Working for a non-profit or mission-driven organisation is sometimes overlooked by job-seekers, often due to beliefs that they are extreme and founded in outdated views. Myths abound such as there will be a smaller operating budget and salaries will be lower. While some of these concerns can play out, there are many benefits from working in non-profit organisations that are not possible to experience in corporate, profit-driven enterprises.

Summary

Research studies exploring people's satisfaction with their work across several domains of study has been conducted and peer-reviewed across many decades. The overwhelming majority of the results demonstrate the positive correlation between work that has a purpose beyond pure profit and employees' sense of satisfaction and contentment.

Deciding to work in an area that has a strong focus on 'giving back to the community' can often mean a sacrifice in pay levels. However, many social enterprises, not-for-profit and community organisations can offer other benefits to their employees, such as more flexible hours, more generous leave entitlements or salary sacrificing benefits.

Ultimately, as an individual, you must decide which aspects of each role will align with your needs and values, and the following tools can assist with your decision.

57

Tools for action

1) Undertake one or more values assessments. These assessments could include the **Schwartz Portrait Values Questionnaire,** which we outlined above. Reflect on the results and how they provide you with some concrete insight into whether you're likely to feel more fulfilled by material benefits or the satisfaction of contributing to the common good.

2) The professional mission worksheet provides a framework for assessing your suitability for purpose-driven employment as well as a list of possible employment categories and job titles to consider. It is available for free at https://www.careeraftercovid.com/missionworksheet

3) Once you have completed the questionnaire and worksheet, spend some time online researching potential roles and organisations that are a good match for your values. Try and find out which positions may fit your skillset, the salary you can expect to uncover if there is possibly an opportunity to pursue a career in a job and workplace that align with your values.

CHAPTER FOUR

MULTIPLY TIME

- -

Strive not to be a success, but rather to be of value.

ALBERT EINSTEIN

Focus on being productive, instead of busy.

TIM FERRIS

Most people would agree that being organised is a positive thing and is something to which we can all aspire. It's a popular business and career topic because of its associations with productivity, success and achievement of goals.

The concepts of getting organised and being productive have gained even more popularity during the pandemic. Dozens of articles have been written about making the most of the lockdown by spring cleaning and getting things in order. It seems like a natural action when you've got the spare time that can come from lockdown.

When Kym and I started the podcast, after we had undertaken our self-assessments, we naturally proceeded to a discussion about getting more organised. It seemed like a clarifying act that would help to counter the unhealthy feelings associated with job loss.

The research literature appears to support our conclusion that being organised assists with health and is an essential component of self-care. A study published in the *Personality and Social Psychology Bulletin* found that women who described their homes as cluttered were more prone to depression, fatigue and higher levels of stress hormones.[14] Clutter is also known to slow down the brain and make it harder to get motivated.

One of the first actions we took was setting a day and time each week to record the podcast remotely via video conference. Since then, we've both remarked on how the simple act of scheduling this regular time has created the structure and organisation around which we have fitted our job search and other activities. We also created space for our work, refreshing tired home offices to help motivate and focus our actions.

---

[14] Saxbe, DE & Repetti, R 2009, 'No place like home: Home tours correlate with daily patterns of mood and cortisol', *Personality and Social Psychology Bulletin*, vol. 36(1), pp. 71–81, <doi:10.1177/0146167209352864.>

Why now is the best time to get organised

The current situation around coronavirus is a stressful time for many. While everyone reacts differently to stressful situations, one of the most common feelings during this time is a sense of helplessness or loss of control. Establishing a routine can help us to feel organised and in control, as well as providing a sense of achievement and accomplishment. Our emotional health can be positively impacted by creating and sticking to this routine.

Our home environment an excellent place to start, in particular getting rid of clutter. While the stacks of newspaper or collections of toys may not feel like a big deal, the constant visual reminders of disorganisation and clutter can drain us and effect on our brains negatively.[15] Essentially, we intrinsically prefer order, and when we can see clutter and mess in our environment, it's distracting. Our cognitive resources and memory suffer, and we find it harder to focus.[16]

61

---

[15] McMains, S & Kastner, S 2011 'Interactions of top-down and bottom-up mechanisms in human visual cortex', *Journal of Neuroscience*, vol.31(2), pp. 587–597, <doi:10.1523/JNEUROSCI.3766-10.2011.>

[16] Gaspar, JM, Christie, JC, Prime, DJ, Jolicoeur, P & McDonald, JJ 2016, 'Inability to suppress salient distractors predicts low visual working memory capacity', Proceedings of the National Academy of Sciences of the United States of America, vol. 113 (13), pp. 3693–98, <https://doi.org/10.1073/pnas.1523471113.>

Living with clutter can eventually lead to more severe issues, such as stress, anxiety and depression. A 2009 research study in the United States demonstrated that levels of the stress hormone cortisol were higher in mothers whose home environment was cluttered.[17]

What does it mean to be organised and productive?

To be organised is to arrange or structure things in a systematic way, enabling the planning of actions and tasks efficiently. As a concept, we often conflate it with being tidy, but organisation takes tidiness one step further. Rather than just tidying those endless piles of paper into neat stacks, being organised involves sorting them systematically to enable the finding of what you need in the least amount of time.

Productivity, in its traditional definition, is 'a way to measure efficiency'. In an economic context, productivity measures the output that comes from units of input. When we talk about productivity in our working and personal lives, we usually mean implementing systems and finding ways to get more done in less time. So, organisation and

[17] Saxbe, DE & Repetti, R 2009, 'No place like home: Home tours correlate with daily patterns of mood and cortisol', *Personality and Social Psychology Bulletin*, vol. 36(1), pp. 71-81, <doi:10.1177/0146167209352864.>

62

productivity naturally go hand in hand when talking about making the most of our time.

Beyond the concept of efficiency is the idea of effectiveness. Kym and I wrote a detailed list of our weekly actions. We realised that a reasonable proportion of our activity was conducted efficiently but was not essentially bringing us closer to our objectives. Our anxious thoughts, caused by job loss, had resulted in us filling up our days with busy work instead of productive work.

Top tips for getting organised and creating good habits

63

If you ask many of my school friends, they will describe me as a very organised person. I'm the one who always remembered birthdays and had a rolling five-year life plan. Once my two children came along, and I moved overseas and back, then across Australia in the space of five years, things got out of sync, and I fell off the organisation wagon.

In recent years, I've been fortunate to meet some remarkable people who have inspired me to be more organised and create some sense of order in my life. It turns out that thoroughly organised people are not born that way. They have to cultivate healthy organisational habits to keep their lives in order, which allows them to live to their full potential and achieve their goals. I'm always hopeful that I can take a growth mindset to any of my actions, and so it's a relief to know that it is possible to learn the critical skill of organisation.

The person who has guided me to a better state of organisation is a Sydney-based organisational expert named Alison Vildos, with the business name 'Aunty Ali'. We met six weeks after I had my second child when I was in the middle of packing up our family home in Sydney, ready for sale. It was an incredibly stressful time, but she made things run smoothly with her combination of organisational nous and empathic pastoral care. After employing Ali from time to time over the years, we have become friends, and I've been fortunate to pick up many great tips and advice from her, some of which I will outline in this chapter. Six years on, and I wouldn't be where I am today without her assistance and support to be organised, confident and more productive.

More than anything else, Ali reminded me to apply the 80/20 rule when setting my objectives for organisation and productivity. I am inclined to spend around 80% of my time on the effort that achieves only 20% of my output. Conversely, 80% of my achievement will come from 20% of focused, goal-oriented activity. The trick has been to carefully analyse my daily efforts using a time-tracking app so I can clearly see which activities are making a difference in reaching my goals, and which ones I should scrap.

Using this time-tracking app has led to me making use of several other technology tools to support my habits and productivity. There are apps and programs available now (many of which are free or low-cost) that enable you to keep track of reaching your goals and achieving your habits. For me, this is a crucial part of staying organised. I derive immense satisfaction from ticking something off my list. Having the right app on my phone means that I know the exact tasks due on a given day.

I'm also a big fan of using an online calendar and making schedules—regular times for specific actions and creating deadlines and due dates for my tasks. I'm realistic enough to recognise that I won't always meet every deadline, but my number one rule is not to miss a deadline more than once. I allow myself flexibility if things turn upside down, to miss one deadline, but my rule means that I have to make an extra effort to ensure a deadline is not missed twice.

Procrastination is an ongoing problem, and it's something that I'm continually working on to overcome. Kym and I discussed some of the techniques we use to overcome procrastination in Episode 8 of the *Career after COVID* podcast. One of my favourites is Kym's technique, borrowed from Mel Robbins' book, *The 5 Second Rule*. Just count down from 5 to 1 and get started. [18]

---

[18] Robbins, M. (2017). *The 5 second rule: Transform your life, work, and confidence with everyday courage.* [Place of publication not identified]: Savio Republic.

Over time, I have also learned to avoid procrastination and distraction by setting aside time each morning to take care of all of the small things that can end up cutting into my deep working time. I've made a list of the actions that I know I gravitate towards to try to avoid doing the complicated, meaningful and productive stuff, and I keep it next to my computer to force me to recognise that activity doesn't necessarily mean effectiveness.

To be able to write and complete this book, I've been crystal clear of my most productive hours. I know that the time between dropping my children at school and lunchtime is my most productive for deep thinking and my creative work. I structure this time to enable two solid hours of deep work every morning, which I supplement with another session later in the day if time permits.

The key actions are:

- Sunday night, every week:
  - o overview and planning for the week ahead, with identification of the tasks that are most likely to result in goal achievement
  - o plan the top three, most-effective actions for the following day, by scheduling them into the diary
  - o explicitly state which activities I will **not** do this week

- Every night:
  - o plan the top three, most-effective actions for the following day, by scheduling them into the diary
  - o go through email inbox and transfer any follow-up actions to my diary, with a set time-limit for completing them.

The pathway to writing this book has enabled me to learn from my authoring mentors just to take action, even if I don't feel like it. And I force myself to just do something towards my book, every single day, even when I'd rather be doing something else or nothing at all. And when I get stuck, I text Kym and request that she counts me down and then I'm straight back to writing.

Over the years, Aunty Ali has also helped me devise some beneficial systems in my home and home office, so I always know where some of the everyday items and implements are stored. The time savings add up when I can put my hand on a roll of sticky tape or an extra charging cord for my phone without a major search operation.

Ali has also supported me to part with some of the sentimentality that I have towards the objects in my life. She coaches me to keep just what I need, rather than stocking up too far in advance. Maintaining this discipline was particularly challenging in the early months of the pandemic. Our natural inclination was to stock up on a range

67

of household items, given the uncertainty of being locked down and the unreliability of stretched supply chains.

Ali has also advised me about the most effective places to discard items that are no longer needed. Sometimes, it was just a case of knowing that someone out there was in more need of my things than I was. I could then let go and create additional space in my home. It also created space in my mind, to take on more important tasks and not be weighed down by the clutter and disorganisation of too much stuff.

Practising delegation is another key strategy that's linked to organisation and productivity. If you have people around you that can support you in learning to let go of some of your tasks, accept their offer of help to lighten your load and reduce your stress levels. Although it was hard in the early days, throughout my career, I've become better at delegating. As someone with a rudimentary knowledge of economics, I think of these matters in terms of opportunity cost. For example, if I can pay someone to make minor updates to my business social media accounts, that gives me time to spend assisting a client or growing my business, which allows me to earn many multiples of that hourly amount potentially.

In Episode 11 of our podcast, we talked about creating good habits and breaking bad habits. One of the concepts that stood out to me in my research of this subject was the way that our habits build over time to create our identity—and how this fact can be reverse engineered to help us have good habits. I had been reading the book, *Atomic Habits* by James Clear, and his example was one person offering two other people a cigarette. One of them responds with, 'Oh no, thanks. I'm trying to quit,' while the other says, 'Oh, no thanks. I'm not a smoker'. Both of these people are trying to quit, but the second one is clearly framing their identity around being a non-smoker. By stating their identity in this way, this person is training their brain to think, behave and form habits that align with their self-identity as a non-smoker.[19]

This example reminded me of how vital self-talk is—words matter in terms of us shaping our own identity. The more you talk about yourself in terms of what you want to be, the easier it is to form habits to get there. It seemed like a very interesting framing of the whole habit concept. When we hear the word 'habit', we get dragged down thinking about the drudge and endless minutiae of habits, without realising that one by one, our practices are forming a big picture of who we are as a person.

Part of being organised and creating good habits can involve engaging an accountability partner to help you get through the tough times when you just want to break your good habits or revert to a bad habit that you've previously

---

[19] Clear, J. Atomic Habits: Tiny Changes, Remarkable Results : An Easy & Proven Way to Build Good Habits & Break Bad Ones. New York: Avery, an imprint of Penguin Random House, 2018.

broken. Training or exercising with a friend is an example of how this strategy can work and keep you accountable. Kym and I work together in this way, keeping each other on track and supporting one another when we drop the ball. Finding a group of like-minded people who are also trying to maintain good habits is a positive way to work towards success.

Another productivity tip we uncovered during our discussions on the podcast, and through our research and reading, was to avoid unnecessary and prolonged meetings as much as possible, particularly in this time of remote work. One of my friends, who is a senior executive in the public service, told me that often she is on video conferences for at least 80% of her day. I suppose that some good work is being done by communicating around the organisation and beyond through these meetings. Still, I'm not sure that a lot of productive work can be happening when people are looking at each other on a screen and talking for that extent of time. If you can influence the scheduling of meetings, always try to suggest that they occur in the afternoons, which for many people is a less productive time and does not take away from the essential deep-thinking morning time.

And finally, learning to say 'no' is a vital part of being organised. One positive to come from the chaos of the pandemic has been an increase in tolerance and acceptance if you're unable to meet the expectations of others. During this challenging time, we have all come to understand the importance of setting boundaries, to look after our mental and physical health. Just like the much-quoted airline safety message, you cannot help others unless you're breathing with your own mask on first.

Pitfalls to avoid

Getting organised is an essential step in the journey to a positive mindset and career security. It's a way to clear your mind for more important tasks and get more out of your time. The only major pitfall to avoid is overdoing it—making organisation an obsession that borders on obsessive-compulsive disorder. It's a comforting trap to fall into, especially in times of flux when our brain and heart may be craving certainty. Strike a balance between utter chaos and organising overwhelm, and you'll be on your way to a more productive and healthy working and home life.

Summary

We've provided an overview of the importance of being organised and the benefits to your productivity and health. Now that we've got our house in order, in the coming chapters, we will explore the process of expanding our minds in terms of career and business options.

71

Tools for action

1) An online or hard copy diary or planner is critical to the process of improving productivity. Use it to set smaller and manageable organisational, productivity and habit goals. Avoid the temptation to overcomplicate the process of getting organised, and don't aim for perfection. If your commitments allow for it, set up a time that is the same every day or week to conquer your decluttering and productivity planning.

2) Consider removing the distractions of technology using . . . technology! Apps such as *AntiSocial* and *SelfControl* help you cut back on social media viewing. *Freedom* and *StayFocused* enable you to prevent internet usage for certain parts of the day when you know you need to be concentrating on something offline.

3) Research and trial some goal-setting apps. Most of them have a free version to trial before upgrading to a paid version with more features. My favourite one is *Todoist*.

As with all of our chapters in this book, we've produced supplementary material that you can access for free, and without the requirement of an email subscription from our website. This material is updated regularly to account for new developments with the virus and in the world of work.

Please see https://www.careeraftercovid.com/ getorganised for a list of available resources.

CHAPTER FIVE

UPSKILL WHAT MATTERS

In a time of drastic change, it is the learners who inherit the future. The learned usually find themselves equipped to live in a world that no longer exists.

ERIC HOFFER

The beautiful thing about learning is that nobody can take it away from you.

B.B. KING

If you've lost your job or been stood down during the coronavirus outbreak, you may be considering enrolling in a university or vocational training course. In this chapter, we talk about the options to consider, and share tips and resources to help you find current course information that is relevant to you.

After we broadcast a podcast episode outlining the range of Commonwealth Government-subsidised short courses, Kym spent time assessing which of these courses would provide her with the best skills and knowledge to propel her career further after the pandemic. At the time of writing, she is close to completing an online *Graduate Certificate in Forensic Psychology* and has shared some of her experience in this chapter.

We have written this chapter with the unemployed or underemployed in mind, rather than those currently employed seeking a career change, or school leavers planning their next study program. We reason that there are many more resources and supports available through Government-funded employment and education programs for those who are currently out of work. This group is likely to be the Government's priority when planning for economic recovery and a return to low unemployment after the worst of the pandemic is over.

Why you should consider study during the pandemic

The decision to start a study pathway is a very individual one. During my many years speaking to thousands of school students about their post-school options, they often asked me, 'Which is the best university?'. My answer was always the same, 'Each university (or degree course) has its advantages and disadvantages, and it's up to every individual to spend the time to find the best university for them'.

It may have seemed like fence-sitting but choosing a pathway that is going to take at least three years of your life and cost you thousands of dollars requires sober research to determine the cost-benefit ratio.

As someone favourable to the concept of life-long learning, I believe the chance to achieve a qualification or gain some new skills while you have time on your hands is one that is worth exploring. In many cases, it's a more comfortable choice to make right now, given the range of free or low-cost courses on offer, many subsidised by Government or not-for-profit agencies as part of a push for economic recovery and greater workplace productivity.

Most of the courses currently on offer to new students are conducted using online learning systems. In-class attendance has been scaled back significantly (or entirely), depending upon where you are in the world. Some online courses are of short duration, and are free or low cost, while others will include a significant time investment, as well as a considerable financial cost. It's essential to research your options carefully and understand whether it will pay dividends in your search for employment when the economy starts to recover.

During a recession, the number of enrolments at universities and vocational education providers usually increase significantly as unemployed people decide to upgrade their skills and prepare for the next economic upswing. Higher education commentator, Dr Andrew Norton noted, 'Recessions change the economics of choosing between higher education and work. If there are no jobs, a university student does not forgo pay and work experience. Higher education's opportunity cost falls. Further study might be the second-best option, but it is better than unemployment." [20]

Kym also observed anecdotally the large number of new students in her graduate certificate course who had taken on this course as a result of being unemployed or underemployed due to COVID.

The professional peer group that you may have been competing with for jobs in the past could emerge from the recession with new qualifications and a range of added skills. As it is in any life endeavour, it helps to have a clear eye on the competition and ensure that you're ready to beat them to the next great opportunity. Therefore, your self-improvement journey through formal study is an activity that is certainly worth prioritising.

[20] Norton, A 2020, Will the COVID-19 recession increase school-leaver applications for higher education?, blog post, 23 March, Andrew Norton, viewed 15 September 2020, <https://andrewnorton.net.au/2020/03/23/will-the-covid-19-recession-increase-school-leaver-applications-for-higher-education/.>

Thinking through which specific outcome you hope to achieve will assist in narrowing down the list of study options. Given the current economic climate, the most appropriate course will be the one that helps your move to a new job or career when the economy picks up.

Some furloughed workers are cutting themselves a little slack and are taking up low-cost courses to fill in time learning something that interests them, while they're not working full time. Even though it might not be job-related, the idea of keeping the brain active is a worthy one.

The flexibility and range of courses on offer, including short courses and micro-degrees, means you can also consider the skills gaps that may be holding you back from finding the job that you genuinely want. If a significant career change is not your goal, find a course that will make you more competitive in your current industry.

Having a clear understanding of your motivation for study and your goal for the end of your studies will help with your decision-making process. If your goal is boosting your current career prospects, then a short course or certificate may be all you need. For those considering moving into a completely different industry, this is likely to require longer-term training and a more considerable investment of money.

It's also essential to do thorough research on the current employment market, and the predictions for the organisations and industries that will be requiring staff in the future. Some of the employment sectors that were predicted to boom before COVID, may or may not continue to have opportunities after the pandemic and associated recession is over.

In September 2020, online job board Seek.com.au published a list of the top twenty most advertised jobs in Australia. They were as follows:

1. Nursing (all roles)
2. Warehousing, Storage & Distribution
3. Aged & Disability Support
4. Automotive Trades
5. Administrative Assistants
6. Sales Representatives/Consultants
7. Physiotherapy, OT & Rehabilitation
8. Childcare & Outside School Hours Care
9. Chefs/Cooks
10. Retail Assistants
11. Developers/Programmers
12. Mining—Engineering & Maintenance
13. Labourers
14. Road Transport
15. Psychology, Counselling & Social Work
16. Dental
17. Child Welfare, Youth & Family Services

18. Plant & Machinery Operators
19. Business / Systems Analysts
20. Mining—Operations[21]

As for future job areas of growth, an August 2020 report from the Australian National Skills Commission shows that data scientists, risk analysts, environmental technicians and biostatisticians are some of the occupations predicted to be sought after in the labour market. The report, which analyses data from the Australian Bureau of Statistics, identifies the twenty-five occupations expected to be in demand in coming years.

These jobs fit into the following industry or skills areas:

- digital deepening—including user experience specialists and social media experts
- data analytics
- business transformation experts such as agile coaches and logistics specialists
- regulatory specialists such as risk analysts and energy auditors
- health practitioners such as nurse liaison officers and biostatisticians

[21] Seek 2020, *20 most-needed jobs*, Seek, Melbourne, viewed 5 October 2020, <https://www.seek.com.au/career-advice/article/australias-most-needed-jobs.>

- sustainability and environmental technical positions
- others, such as fundraisers and researchers.[22]

When Kym and I moved into a period of employment uncertainty, we invested time in gaining a deep understanding of our current skills, and the skills we might need to land our next role. As well as job and industry-specific skills and knowledge, we also considered which generic skills are in demand by employers and whether we need to develop those skills. Generic or soft skills include skills such as written and verbal communication, empathy, resilience and reliability.

The other consideration is whether there are particular industry accreditations or licenses that are needed. Furthermore, are there formal qualifications that are regulated by specific industries such as accounting, teaching or nursing?

Once you have narrowed down the skills and type of course you need, you can start comparing providers. Look at the ratings that have been given by graduates of the courses that you're thinking of undertaking. If possible, speak to students currently enrolled to get a clearer idea of the

---

[22] National Skills Commission 2020, *25 Emerging Occupations*, report, National Skills Commission, Canberra, viewed 11 September 2020, <https://www.nationalskillscommission. gov.au/25-emerging-occupations.>

quality of the learning environment and the outcomes that students have achieved. Treat your study as any other type of financial investment by ensuring that it will be right for you and that you will benefit from the outlay of your money and time.

Pitfalls to avoid

It is common for adults who performed poorly at high school to believe that they are not suited to adult education. If you are carrying these restricting self-beliefs, be aware the two are vastly different. If you lack confidence, start slow and take advantage of the student advice and support resources that most course providers offer. You could also sign up for a low-cost short course or taster course to get a sense of how student life may fit around your other commitments.

83

While you may feel a sense of urgency to select a study pathway while there is time on your side, it's better to take the time to research so that you can choose the course that will deliver the best return on your investment.

Summary

In this chapter, you discovered a range of ways you can upskill while you may have additional time on your hands during the economic downturn. In the chapter that follows, we launch head-first into the process of validating your business idea and getting it off the ground.

Tools for action

1) If you haven't already done so, utilise the tools listed at the end of Chapters Two and Three to gain deeper insights into possible career paths, which will in turn help to inform your study path.

2) Once you have a shortlist of potential courses, visit the Australian Government's Course Seeker website (courseseeker.edu.au) to see detailed information on course structures, career pathways and institutional and course ratings to help you to choose. If you have further questions and wish to talk to someone, all education providers employ prospective student advisers to assist with course selection,

3) If you're unsure of where to turn, post a question in Career after COVID's *Career Rockstars* Facebook or LinkedIn groups, and we will try to help you with your course query.

As with all of our chapters in this book, we've produced supplementary material that you can access for free, and without the requirement of an email subscription, from our website. This material is updated regularly to account for new research and developments.

Please see https://www.careeraftercovid.com/ courses for a list of available resources.

CHAPTER SIX

OUTSIDE-THE-BOX THINKING FOR CASH GENERATION

The ultimate purpose of money is so that you do not have to be in a specific place at a specific time doing anything you don't want to do.

NAVAL RAVIKANT

Stop buying things you don't need to impress people you don't even like.

SUZE ORMAN

This chapter is short and action-focused. It's about finding ways to expand your income sources, enabling more time to prepare for the next stage of your career or business journey. Hopefully, you are or have recently been receiving a government benefit if you're unemployed, meaning you do have some form of income support. If you're struggling to put food on the table or access accommodation, then please access the resources that may be available to you. We have compiled a list on our website careeraftercovid. com that we hope will assist, and we will continue to update the resources and information as things change. Otherwise, we assume that you've got enough money to survive the day-to-day and that a little bit extra could help propel your career in a new direction.

If you're thinking about setting up a new business as your next move, an online business can be started for as little as a few hundred dollars and be earning income for you within weeks. With a few of the ideas in this chapter, you can have your business set-up fund underway.

Why is it essential to find additional income sources? Shouldn't I concentrate on finding a new job?

The relatively generous Government benefits will not be available forever, and it's critical to prepare early to maximise your options. Government agencies and the Reserve Bank are predicting that the economy will be in a recession well into 2021. The opportunities to take on new jobs will be limited until there's a full recovery.

It's easy to get caught up in the mindset that you're flat broke and can't move forward because of a lack of funds.

You could be missing out on the funding source that could take your employment journey to a new level of success. The pandemic has been a crisis, but out of these difficult times, many great careers and businesses have started. You don't want to miss out on the uptick that will come with economic recovery.

How can I earn additional income during the pandemic?

This chapter will outline some ideas that are career-related and involve skills development or resume building and others that are just pure money-making to get your bank balance in a position for you to plan for your future sensibly.

Before you get started, however, we suggest you undertake a simple exercise to calculate what an hour or your time is worth. It's then possible to use one of the time-tracking apps to understand your time investment in each project. Essentially, I've always been able to work out my nominal hourly opportunity cost by dividing my annual income by the number of hours I worked in a year. As an example, if I was earning $80,000 per year, I divided this by 52 weeks (even though I only worked 48 because of annual leave, I was still remunerated based on 52 weeks) then divided by 37.5, which was the number of hours I was expected to work each week.

$$\$80,000 / 52 / 37.5 = \$41 \text{ per hour}$$

I then knew what an hour of my time was worth before I paid tax on it, and therefore strived to spend my time in such a way that I wasn't earning less than that amount unless there was some other non-financial benefit involved. It's always been a helpful way for me to allocate my time resources.

Selling physical items

Some of the ways that you can potentially earn extra money include selling physical items that you already own, such as excess household items that are no longer needed. If you have the skillset or are willing to learn, you could also try your hand at making or crafting items to sell.

According to Gumtree's 2019 Second-hand Economy Report, 89% of Australian households have unwanted items they could sell, worth an average of $5,300 per household.[23] Even if your home has just half of that amount, it could provide options in terms of investment in a new business idea, or some tools or education to help your career go further.

One of the oldest business models in the world is the 'arbitrage' or 'buy low, sell high' model. If you're able to source an item at a much lower cost than you know you can sell it for, the difference between the two becomes your

---

[23] Gumtree 2020, Second hand economy report, Gumtree, Sydney, viewed 10 August 2020, <https://www.gumtree.com.au/second-hand-economy-report/.>

income. Kym has started an online second-hand denim store with this principle in mind. She sources and curates a retail supply of jeans and other denim items and styles and promotes them with enough of a margin to justify the time she spends on the business.

Another idea that is steadily gaining traction is to sell items online using techniques such as drop-shipping.

Drop-shipping is a popular new retail model that many people who set up their own business for the first time are attracted to because of its low entry costs. It's also a perfect business model for working from home. The basic premise is that you act as an intermediary for a supplier or manufacturer by setting up a website to promote and sell products. Once orders are taken, they are forwarded to your supplier for fulfilment and shipping.

Drop-shipping tends to work best for novelty items, apparel and accessories that can be inexpensively manufactured overseas. Pet products and hard-to-find technical spare parts are two examples of niches that have seen good results in the past.

Finding a niche and then testing a range of products is one of the most time-consuming parts of the process for most drop-shippers. Once your item or items gain traction, it is relatively easy to scale the business.

A complicating factor during COVID is the blow-out of shipping times due to decreased air freight activity, so it is imperative to manage your customers' expectations on your website. Potential drop-shippers also need to be aware of the downsides of this business model, including the high levels of competition (and corresponding low margins), and relative lack of control of essential business components including quality control, shipping times and your business' brand.

Print-on-demand is another option, where you pay a printer to print your design on an item of apparel or novelty item (stickers, mugs and so forth). Once the item is ordered on your website by the purchaser, you pay the printer, and the item is sent directly to the buyer. The difference between the cost and sale price is your gross profit. Print-on-demand has similar downsides as drop-shipping.

Selling digital content

Creating content and monetising it is an income-generation tool that has gained further popularity during the pandemic. Suppose you have a subject area that you are incredibly knowledgeable and passionate about. In that case, there is bound to be an audience of potentially hundreds or thousands of people somewhere in the world with a similar interest, who may become your loyal readers or listeners. You could consider writing a blog or recording a podcast about your area of interest. Once you have built an audience, your content may have income-generating possibilities.

The two most popular sources are affiliate commissions from providers who pay you a small percentage for referring buyers to their websites and products, and advertisers who run commercial messages within your content.

Online courses, a subset of the digital content category, have become a significant source of business growth during the pandemic as people spend more time at home and wish to improve their skills. If you have a skillset to share or knowledge to convey, creating an online course is worth considering. The range of offerings has expanded well beyond the predictable technology and software training courses, with experts around the world making money teaching music, baking, art and other skills.

When done right, online education has the potential to not only create income but also to boost your credibility as an expert in your field. It's also a very scalable business model. *Teachable* and *Udemy* are two platforms that online educators are using to set up and promote their courses.

Writing an e-book, which is a small downloadable book, can be an effective way to build an email list for your existing business. Most businesses offer it for free in exchange for an email address, which creates communications and sales possibilities. You will hear many entrepreneurs say that their email list is one of their most valuable business assets. Remember, your social media pages and profiles are not your property and can be shut down without notice.

An email list is a tangible asset that cannot be taken away from you, provided you keep it secure and use it ethically.

Selling creative content

If you're talented with a camera, you could sell your photos or video clips to stock libraries such as *Alamy* and get a small income from people who download your images. Narrating audiobooks is another example of monetising creative content.

Providing services in person, or remotely

You may consider offering your services, for example, as a virtual assistant, and earn income assisting busy people in organising themselves. You can take on small tasks through technologies and apps like *Airtasker* or via freelance services such as *Upwork, Fiverr* or *freelancer.com*. If you have an academic background or in-depth knowledge of a subject or field, you could also potentially offer online tutoring.

Miscellaneous ways to get paid

There's also a range of miscellaneous options for earning an extra income if you know where to look. These include income sources such as being paid to undertake surveys or work as a secret shopper providing companies with feedback on their customer service. You might even sign up to take part in medical research and be paid to trial a new drug or therapy. Of course, choose these options with caution. Only work with reputable organisations and be sure you always read the fine print before you register.

Pitfalls to avoid

It's a good idea to ensure there is a positive return on investment for the time you spend trying to make 'quick' money. Use the 'opportunity cost calculator' mentioned in this chapter's introduction to ensure you get value back from the time you commit.

Summary

This chapter has provided a brief overview of how you can earn extra income while the pandemic has curtailed your primary source of income. The key to adding to your income sources is to master the skills of observation and creative problem-solving. The more you engage with the world around you, whether that be through media consumption, social media networking or observing people in person, the more likely you will be to see a need for a solution that people will pay for. Always be on the lookout.

95

Tools for action

1) Identify your strengths: Start with a brainstorm, thinking about the things you like to do, including your hobbies. Perhaps you have a creative streak and can make something that is in high demand right now. Or maybe you have specialist knowledge in a field that you could monetise with a blog or a podcast.

   Be confident in asking around to see if people in your social or professional network need assistance. It is possible to build a successful business providing necessary administrative support as a virtual executive assistant. Word can spread fast through real-life interactions with friends and family, as well as your social networks.

2) Research task marketplaces: If you're planning on offering a product or service online and are not sure how to advertise it, use one of the online marketplaces to start you off. I recently checked Fiverr.com and was amazed at the range of tasks people will pay for. Not big money, but money,

nonetheless. People are receiving US$5 to take a photo of themselves wearing a company's t-shirt!

3) Sell what you don't need: It's a good idea to do a thorough search of your home and find all of the unwanted goods that you could sell online. From there, research the amount these items are selling for in online marketplaces, like Gumtree, eBay or Facebook marketplace.

In addition to the steps above, we've produced supplementary material that you can access for free from our website. There is also a comprehensive list of places you can access support and financial assistance if you are in need. This material is updated regularly to account for new research and developments.

You can access the latest resources here: https://www.careeraftercovid.com/makemoney.

PART TWO

BACK IN THE GAME

CHAPTER SEVEN

THE NEW WORLD OF HIRING

Train people well enough so they can leave. Treat them well enough, so they don't want to.

SIR RICHARD BRANSON

101

It's no secret that the jobs market and how organisations hire staff members have changed significantly as a result of the restrictions on person-to-person contact as well as the fluctuations in the economy as a whole. Depending on the industry, the changes to recruitment have been broad and deep, including the places that organisations are advertising (or not advertising) open positions, the way staff are selected, the power differential between employer and candidate, and the onboarding process for new hires.

In this brief, descriptive chapter, we provide an overview of the main ways that recruitment has changed during the pandemic, based on our discussions with colleagues in the HR and recruitment industry. The following two chapters will provide the practical advice you need to capitalise on these changes and ensure you're a strong candidate for the job you want.

How are organisations' hiring practices different now?

Significant changes have occurred in recruitment have due to social distancing requirements, mandated by law in most countries for at least some of the pandemic period. In turn, these distancing requirements have forced organisations to rethink their application of technology. Staff recruitment practises have not been immune from the 'fast-tracking' of remote networking, automation and machine learning that has been imperative for organisations to keep operating during the lockdowns.

These developments have resulted in economic and industry changes, which have in turn been exacerbated by wide-scale fluctuations in consumer and business confidence as the pandemic has progressed and spread. In a large number of industries and organisations, there has been a corresponding loss in revenue—but there are also many 'good news stories' that have emerged of organisations having their busiest and most profitable year ever as a result of COVID.

Bill Boorman is an experienced recruiter based out of the United Kingdom, and his insights on the changes to the methods by which organisations recruit and hire talent are as follows:

- The video interview and online recruitment and selection process are widespread and here to stay.
- The length of time it takes to recruit is around 45–50% shorter than before COVID, aided by the online process. Some recruiters indicated that hiring managers were dealing with so much change elsewhere in their businesses; they wanted the recruitment of new staff to be as smooth and straightforward a process as possible.
- Organisations can consider hiring on a broader geography for specialist roles, given the ability or imperative to offer work from home roles in many industries.
- Executive-level permanent hiring is recovering slower than temporary, contract, blue-collar and junior staff recruitment activity. Organisations are still unsure of the economic outlook and have been reticent to commit to significant hires in many industries. There is a mismatch between candidates' desire for certainty and security and organisations' risk aversion when it comes to hiring.[24]

103

---

[24] Boorman, B 2020, The HRChat Podcast, accessed 25 September 2020.

The approach that candidates take to their career management (the how, why and will they seek new opportunities) and their expectations of the hiring organisation have also changed in the following ways:

- Many professionals have reassessed their career trajectory, what motivates them and what they expect from their next role. In-demand candidates (especially in areas of skill shortage) are likely to raise their expectations of hiring organisations throughout the recruitment process as well as the overall employment brand and benefits.
- Candidates are less interested in the 'bean bag and ping-pong table' working environment and are seeking workplace satisfaction through other means.

According to the Australian Bureau of Statistics' *September 2020 Labour Force Statistics* report, there were 937,000 unemployed people in Australia, a 32.2% increase on September 2019.[25] Deloitte Access Economics predicts the unemployment rate will remain high until 2024, rising to 8.3 per cent in 2021-22 before slowly declining to 7.6 per cent in 2022-23, 6.8 per cent in 2023-24 and 6.2 per cent in 2024-25. The rate in 2019-20 was 5.6 per cent.

104

---

[25] Australian Bureau of Statistics 2020, Labour Force, Australia, accessed 20 October 2020.

As for the job market, according to online job board Seek in October 2020, accounting job ads had declined by almost 44 per cent, legal jobs ads by 43 per cent, IT job ads by 38 per cent, and sales job ads by 30 per cent.[26]

There will be many more job-seekers for every role available than in pre-COVID times, increasing the pressure on candidates to stand out from competing applicants. Added to this is the pressure on recruiters to wade through dozens, hundreds or maybe even thousands of job applications for each role.

Technology will play an ever-expanding part in candidate identification and selection, which is why the advice in the next two chapters is required reading for anyone wanting to move into a new position during the pandemic and its immediate aftermath.

Applicant Tracking Systems (ATSs) are commonplace in all large organisations and many small to medium enterprises, and the use of algorithms to filter job applicants to a shortlist must be taken into account when applying for jobs in 2020 and beyond. We will explore the implications of this in Chapter Nine.

Bill Boorman also pointed to recruiters having to refine their algorithms to account for the growing proportion of

---

[26] Seek.com.au newsletter, accessed 20 October 2020

job candidates switching industries. In the past, recruiters may have set their algorithm to favour candidates with similar employment histories in terms of job title and industry. In the middle of this global crisis, recruiters are broadening their conception of an ideal candidate. They are considering how the skills of currently redundant sectors, such as aviation and tourism, can be re-engaged for the benefit of employers in other parts of the economy. Policy-makers have also started tapping into the potential for workers to transfer between industries, so it looks set to be an opportunity to watch.

Summary

The changes to recruitment that have been brought on by the pandemic are widespread, and most of them are here to stay. As a current job-seeker, a knowledge of these changes will guide you in your application process and likely improve your chances of gaining an interview.

The following two chapters reflect these changes and are action-oriented to ensure you can capitalise on the new recruitment landscape.

Tools for action

1) Sign up for the recruitment industry and workplace newsletters that will keep you informed of developments in the job-hunting sphere. Kym and I are regular site visitors or subscribers to the following updates and have found them useful:

   - Australian Financial Review Work and Careers (https://www.afr.com/work-and-careers)

   - Seek.com.au news (https://www.seek.com.au/about/news/)

   - LinkedIn Get Hired Australia (https://www.linkedin.com/pulse/introducing-get-hired-australia-newsletter-job-hunters-cayla-dengate/).

CHAPTER EIGHT

LINKEDIN AS AN INDISPENSABLE CAREER AND BUSINESS TOOL

LinkedIn is no longer an online resume. It's your digital reputation.

JILL ROWLEY

Kym and I discussed LinkedIn on Episode 6 of the *Career after COVID* Podcast, and it was one of our most popular episodes.

Many people are still sceptical about LinkedIn based on what they knew of it many years ago. It was rather uninspiring and easy to disparage as an online CV repository and a place where random strangers send you messages on the anniversary of you starting at your current job. Many of the most active users cross the line between being informative and blatantly self-promotional, therefore striking a balance between communicating your professional value and becoming boorish is key to optimising LinkedIn's value. With the tips we outline below, you'll be able to use LinkedIn to learn, grow and connect, whether you are a business owner, currently employed or searching for work.

Why do I need LinkedIn?

LinkedIn has a global user base of more than 700 million people.[27] We've now reached the point, especially in light of how many people are unemployed, that LinkedIn is becoming essential to almost all job search activity.

LinkedIn is a useful platform to research potential employers, and it has also developed into a pathway for others to find you online very successfully. If you search for a professional contact's name online, you will usually find that their LinkedIn profile is the top or nearly-top result. In this way, LinkedIn has become a powerful search engine in its own right. This reason alone is why all working people and prospective working people (e.g., students) need to have a profile on this platform. LinkedIn has progressively reached beyond its white-collar and business owner beginnings

---

[27] Extrapolations of data from LinkedIn's self-service advertising tools (July 2020)

and is embracing membership and activity by blue-collar workers as well.

Since Microsoft purchased LinkedIn in 2016, there have been several new features added, such as a section indicating to recruiters that you're searching for work, without your connections and contacts being aware. You can also showcase your top pieces of work, and for business owners, you can include a featured list of services or products that you offer.

Another powerful tool is the ability to highlight a variety of posts that you've created on LinkedIn or other platforms so that viewers of your profile see the type of content you want them to focus on, right at the top of your profile.

LinkedIn is not just for professionals and job-seekers; it's for business owners as well. If you've decided to launch a business, you can create a LinkedIn business page that links from your personal page. It's another way to get the name of your business seen by more people, and it can give your emerging small business more credibility as it's being established.

How to develop an 'all-star' LinkedIn profile

When it comes to your profile, it's essential that the information is current and that every section supports the achievement of your career goals.

Your profile picture and headline

These are the two most important pieces of online real estate in your profile, and both need to be used for maximum effect. Your profile picture should be a recent, crisp, professional photograph (preferably a headshot) that conveys you in a positive light.

Your headline returns the most value if it's a catchy, action-oriented statement about what you offer or what you're aspiring to, rather than merely the default mention of your current position and employer. Using your current position as the headline is wasting a valuable opportunity because you're duplicating the current position information that anyone can just scroll down and see. You need to sell with the headline and focus on your career goals and values that you're espousing in your professional life.

As an example, a friend of our family aspires to work in urban planning. She has completed a built environment degree and is in the early stages of her career. When we set up her LinkedIn profile together, I suggested she use the headline, 'Aspiring Urban Planner' rather than 'Built Environment Graduate'.

This idea works on the principle of 'If you build it, they will come' - if you put it out there, LinkedIn users searching using those keywords are more likely to find you. In the same way that keywords in headings on web pages help search engines find relevant content, your LinkedIn headline is the place where you'll achieve networking and job-seeking success from using keywords that align with your goals. Ensure that your headline indicates the types of career specialisations or skill areas that you're planning to target with your next, or subsequent career move.

If you're unemployed, in our view it's best not to write 'Seeking new opportunities.' Consider including a statement that you're aspiring to be in a particular role or industry. A potential employer will scroll down and see that you may not be currently employed. Like many aspects of life in the pandemic, however, people are far more forgiving, considering that so many people have lost jobs through no fault of their own.

It took a while for both of us to feel comfortable revealing our unemployed status on our profiles, but who knows where it might lead if you're open about your situation.

Your keywords

The use of appropriate and effective keywords in your LinkedIn profile is critical. In my case, when I was working for the blockchain start-up, I didn't lead with 'Director of Marketing and PR' as my headline. Instead, I wrote 'Blockchain

Marketing Strategist', and I received so many messages from people seeking me out for blockchain-related comment, including a member of the Commonwealth parliament, because I had that word in my headline. I got invited to speak at an international conference and had a magazine profile published, highlighting my role as an Australian woman in the blockchain and cryptocurrency space. When you're using relevant and goal-oriented keywords in your profile, you may find that you get approached for all sorts of opportunities.

You should also use as many words as you can when filling out each of your role descriptions in the profile section. However, it's important not to stuff these descriptions with too many keywords so that it becomes hard to read.

Your cover photograph

Apart from your profile photo, there's an opportunity to use the cover photo, which you can create on a design software platform like Canva so that it is the right size for your LinkedIn profile. This visual cue further highlights something about you, your interests, your skills, or more importantly, your career direction or goals. If you're operating your own business, it can even have a call to action to enable viewers to link directly to a lead magnet on your business website.

Kym and I have worked in organisations where we had the option of using the company's branded cover page for our LinkedIn page, to create a unified look for the staff members of that organisation. If it's not mandatory, you should consider using your own cover image that projects your goals and interests in a unique way.

Your LinkedIn summary

Think of this space as somewhere to give added voice to your personal statement from your CV. Use the full word count to form an image in the mind of the viewer about your career trajectory and the skills and experience you offer. Along with your entire profile, the summary should reflect your career goals. In essence, it is supposed to be your sales pitch or 'elevator pitch,' so make it count.

I often get asked by clients if they should write the summary section in the first or third person. My recommendation is to write it in the first person because it is your profile, and readers will know that you are writing it. It also creates a sense of connection and warmth.

Your personal information

It's appropriate to mention your hobbies and the types of things that you spend time on outside of work. Doing so humanises you, and so long as it doesn't take away from what your career direction is, it can end up attracting you, via the magic of keywords, to people who share similar interests.

Gaps in your employment history

Our recommendation is to be open and honest about any gaps or career breaks. A study from Australian online employment site Seek.com.au shows that employers prefer not having to guess why these gaps occurred.[28] Consider the activities that you undertook during these periods, and create timeline entries that reflect these activities, such as study, personal development, travel or family caring responsibilities.

You may consider establishing a sole trader, side-hustle or freelance business early in your career, as a role to fall back on in between other jobs that you undertake. Having a business name that becomes your vehicle for freelance work is an ideal solution to explaining any gaps, especially now in the time of coronavirus. It also shows that you've taken the initiative of setting up your own enterprise.

As an example, I set up my marketing consulting activities as a sole trader in 2006. That business has kept me occupied in between other activities, including child-rearing and family caring responsibilities.

Your role descriptions

I advise writing a summary for each role, highlighting duties and significant achievements, who you've reported to, the number of staff members you've managed and your

---

28

budget responsibilities. Two or three paragraphs for each role is more than adequate unless it was a junior casual job while you were at university. It is a chance to expand on your position and the skills that you have developed, and to have some of those things picked up by keyword searches.

I strongly encourage LinkedIn users to include as much data as they can when describing their achievements. Remember, the physical CV that you send directly to employers has to be short and concise. LinkedIn is the opportunity to highlight the accomplishments of your career thus far, so quantify achievements as much as possible.

For example, you might say:

- during the four years I spent recruiting students, enrolments at my university more than tripled
- I led the project team whose implementation resulted in a 7% increase in student satisfaction
- customer returns decreased by 42% as a direct result of the strategies my team implemented during my time in retail.

Projects, skills and test scores

The other part of your profile that is significant is the project section. Complete this with the details of particular projects that you worked on within your various roles. Any time you undertake a project of any type that may be of interest to a future employer or client, include it in this section. Link the project with the colleagues that you worked with to add credibility to what you undertook.

So, for example, you might include:

- coordination of an international research delegation
- management of a successful government grant application
- facilitating the development of an organisation's strategic plan.

Add a couple of paragraphs that explain the project and what the project involved in terms of skills, as well as the quantified results. There are numerous options for including projects to bulk up your profile and add to your searchability.

LinkedIn also provides options to include test scores and certifications that you've received. In the courses section, I've outlined all of the subjects that I undertook as part of my undergraduate and postgraduate study, to show the breadth of what I've undertaken and to be found more easily in searches.

The skills section is especially important, as it is this list that the LinkedIn algorithm uses to suggest possible jobs to you. There's a section for highlighting up to fifty of your skills, so consider using as many as possible, if they are legitimate skills you hold. As you develop in your career, make a point of endorsing others for the skills that you know they have, and hopefully they will reciprocate with an endorsement of the skills that they know you have.

Your recommendations

By writing recommendations for people that you've worked with, you will hopefully encourage them to write one back for you. Written references have become a thing of the past in job-seeking these days. The LinkedIn model of endorsements and recommendations is a public way to provide social proof of your achievements, skills and way of working.

Consider providing recommendations and endorsements for your peers and the people reporting to you. It's also appropriate to offer an endorsement of the management style of your superiors and the leaders in your organisation. It's a professional compliment for leaders to be given feedback about the things that they did well. If they choose to add your recommendation to their profile, it's likely to assist both of you in your career trajectories.

Your updates

Once your profile is set up, you can start to attract followers and build networks by posting updates and using hashtags. Posting original content is ideal, but reposting and sharing updates from others along with your comments or opinion is also useful. For example:

- Here's a great Lean Canvas template created by Acme Corporation that I wanted to share to assist with your #businessplanning. #strategy #leanstartups
- This recent tweet from the CEO of Bloggs Inc resonated with me in these challenging times. #covid #motivation

The use of hashtags in your posts can further extend the reach of your content to users who are following those hashtags. For example, at the time of writing, #innovation had more than 37 million followers worldwide, #leanstartups had more than 19 million and #motivation had more than 13 million.

According to LinkedIn's statistics from 2019, content on the LinkedIn feed receives about 9 billion impressions per week. Only 3 million users (out of the more than 500 million) share content every week. These statistics show that only about 1% of LinkedIn's 260 million monthly users share posts, and those 3 million or so users net the 9 billion impressions. That's an average of 3000 impressions per active user per week. It stands to reason that you have the opportunity to advance your professional authority and career progress by tapping into all of those eyeballs.

Pitfalls to avoid

It sounds obvious, but it's so important to check for typographical and grammatical errors meticulously. Kym and I check each other's profiles as an extra step with a set of fresh eyes. A LinkedIn profile with mistakes and spelling errors creates a negative first impression for a prospective employer or client.

Summary

As you can tell from this chapter's content, we are great believers in the potential of LinkedIn as a career and business tool. Even though LinkedIn was founded two years before Facebook, there are still many sceptics who underestimate its power and authority as THE professional networking platform.

Given the generosity of LinkedIn's algorithm in terms of sharing organic content, even a moderate investment of your time in updating and expanding your profile, plus posting or responding to others' posts occasionally, is sure to have an impact on your prospects and career trajectory.

Tools for action

1) If you don't already have a LinkedIn profile, create one. Then start connecting with colleagues, and insert as many of the elements discussed in this chapter to create an all-star profile.

2) Follow LinkedIn on LinkedIn (and other social media platforms) to be kept up to date with developments on their platform.

3) Commit to writing one recommendation per month for someone you've worked with. Hopefully they will return the favour, and if they don't, feel free to ask!

As with all of our chapters in this book, we've produced supplementary material that our valued readers can access for free, and without the requirement for an email subscription, from our website. This material is updated regularly to account for new research and developments.

Please see https://www.careeraftercovid.com/ linkedin for a list of available resources.

122

CHAPTER NINE

GET AHEAD OF THE COMPETITION

- -

Be so good they can't ignore you.

STEVE MARTIN

How to be the number one candidate for a job and get hired is perhaps the fundamental question this book seeks to answer for you. We don't need to convince you of the importance of this chapter, because it's the reason you're reading this book. Therefore, we will get straight to the how-to of finding and being hired for the right job during the pandemic and the economic aftershocks.

The objective of this chapter is to provide immediately actionable advice for your job hunt that is relevant to the economic downturn and health-related restrictions that we currently face. So much of the general advice on this subject is common sense, and there are myriad sources of tips and hacks available with a simple online search, so we have honed this information down to the key things that will influence your ability to get hired during and after COVID-19.

Many of our podcast listeners report that they're finding jobs to apply for, but are feeling dejected at the thought of competing with hundreds of other applicants. If you're in the same situation, we recommend that you consider revisiting Chapter One of this book and using some of those tools and ideas to re-gain career confidence and a positive mindset.

Also, as mentioned in the tools for action section at the end, there are several useful references, templates and 'cheat sheets' available from our website, most of them free to download.

The process of getting hired during COVID

We provided an overview of the way the recruitment market and process has changed in response to the pandemic in Chapter Seven. However, the critical elements of a job search and hiring process largely remain the same (although some have changed format or mode of execution) and are as follows:

- your resume or Curriculum Vitae (CV)
- your cover letter and additional documentation

- your LinkedIn and other online profiles and references
- the interview.

In my experience as a recruiter and hiring manager, reviewing more than 3000 applications for more than 100 roles, I've always approached the hiring process as follows:

1. Fundamentally, it's a two-way sales and marketing process, with the odds usually stacked in favour of the employer. The candidate has to sell themselves as a person that will assist the organisation, and the hiring manager, in meeting their objectives.
2. Secondly, from the point of view of the employer, it is a risk-minimisation process. If you've spent any time working in an organisation, you're highly likely to remember an instance of the wrong person being selected for a position. What is often more memorable is the cost of this mistake for an organisation, in terms of lost productivity and potentially, decreased staff morale for the other employees.

Therefore, as you approach your job search, you should keep the perspective of the hiring manager and organisation at the forefront of everything you communicate, online and in person.

Your Resume or CV—what's the difference?

We discussed CVs and resumes in Episode 21 of the *Career after COVID* Podcast and provided tips based on our experience as hiring managers and, more recently, job applicants during the pandemic.

In Australia, the terms, 'resume' and 'Curriculum Vitae' (CV) tend to be used interchangeably to describe the document a job applicant presents to a prospective employer to outline their career and education trajectory, as well as fundamental and specialist skills.

In academic circles and some other parts of the world, a resume is a brief (1-2 page) outline of experience and skills relevant to the current job being applied for, while a CV is a longer-form document providing detail of all of your education and employment history.

If you're not sure which type of document is required, it's a good idea to check with the recruiter or hiring manager to ensure you are presenting your background in the correct format. There is no one-size-fits-all format, but at the bare minimum, you should include:

Personal details, such as name and contact details.

A personal statement (also known as a branding statement) that succinctly states your career objective, strengths and concrete, quantified achievements. Effective

126

personal statements are focused on the goals or pain points of the hiring organisation and make the reader want to find out more about you. Here is a recent personal statement of mine:

I thrive in high-pressure business situations and feel most fulfilled when I have played a role in assisting people and organisations to reach their potential. I've grown revenue by more than 300% at a complex, multi-site organisation and led the strategy to achieve double-digit year-on-year increases in 5-star customer satisfaction reviews.

Employment experience (reverse chronological order), ensuring you list significant achievements for each role, with data to back up your claims

Education (reverse chronological order). Mention principal areas of study that are relevant to the job and provide academic transcripts separately if requested

Skills, including hard skills, technology platforms and software you are skilled in using. I list them in a table format in my CV that makes my level of skill clear and how recently or how often I use this skill, as follows:

Technology skills

Skill	Level	Usage
Microsoft Word	Advanced	Daily, current
Microsoft Project	Intermediate	Weekly, until mid-2019
HTML	Basic	Daily, until 2017

Workplace and soft skills

Skill	Level	Usage
Workshop facilitation	Advanced	Monthly, until early 2018
SEO copywriting	Advanced	Weekly, current

Provide names of **referees** if requested. Otherwise, a simple statement at the end stating, 'names can be provided on request' is adequate.

Your CV or resume and cover letter are essentially marketing documents and a sales pitch that convinces the employer that you have the required skills, attitude and background for the role. Beyond the essential criteria, it is critical to highlight your 'unfair advantage' or 'unique selling point' that makes you the best candidate.

Applicant Tracking Systems (ATS)

COVID has meant more and more organisations are using AI (artificial intelligence) recruitment tools such as ATS (applicant tracking systems) to help compile a shortlist for interview and reduce the workload for the selection committee. An algorithm, rather than a human, is used to make the first cull of applications. As you may know, algorithms often crawl documents to find keywords to help them make decisions.

The job advertisement, job description, list of selection criteria and any supplementary documentation provided to applicants are highly likely to contain the keywords that the algorithm is programmed to search for and decide whether a candidate proceeds to Stage Two. Use the same keywords for skills and experience as those listed in the job advertisement.

As an example, if the advertised role is for an executive assistant, ensure that your CV lists your most recent position using these words, even if that wasn't your specific job title. Your most recent roles may have been 'personal assistant' or 'administrative assistant' positions, in which case you could convey this as follows:

Jan 2020 - Sep 2020

Employer: Acme Corporation

Position: Administrative Assistant (working closely with an executive assistant)

Duties: Provision of administrative assistance to senior managers

In the above brief example, I've included the keyword 'executive assistant' in the position name while ensuring that I represent the role faithfully and honestly. It's not a guaranteed method to get through the first round of machine selection but gives you an idea of how you can sensibly weave relevant keywords into your application.

Other tips to consider

Here are our top tips for catching the attention of the recruiter and conveying your employability in each of your CV and cover letter:

- Keep your CV and cover letter uncluttered, no more than one or two A4 pages each (unless requested otherwise in the job advertisement) and make every word count. The CV and cover letter are designed to get you an interview first and foremost.
- Tailor it to the job and organisation and focus intently on the organisation's objectives, values, culture and how you can resolve their challenges. It's important not to cut and paste from other job applications.
- Address the cover letter to the hiring manager or recruiter listed in the advertisement, rather than writing 'Dear Sir/Madam.' A search on the organisation's webpage or LinkedIn should be enough to find the correct addressee if it has not been included in the job listing.
- Focus on what makes you unique—your unfair advantage over other candidates.

- Show enthusiasm, energy, willingness to learn (learning agility) and desire to succeed.
- Use data where possible to prove your skills or experience.
- And always, always proofread!

The Interview

Here are the four things on my must-do list when I attend a job interview, which apply equally for in-person and remote, video-linked interviews:

1. I prepare thoroughly by knowing precisely what is in the job advertisement, what I've written in my application, who might be on the interviewing panel and the latest news for the organisation and its major competitors and stakeholders (using their webpage and a Google news search). If technology is involved, I ensure this is tested well in advance.

2. I research possible questions using an online search and prepare answers. I also prepare two or three questions to ask the interviewer or panel. We've compiled a list of our favourites in the tools section of our website.

3. I start the interview remembering the number one thing for all my public speaking engagements: this audience or panel **wants** me to do a good job. They are on my side; they **want** me to be a great candidate worthy of employment so they can complete the

131

recruitment process. This tactic calms my nerves immediately.

4. I smile and provide eye contact throughout the interview to every panel member, no matter how nervous I am.

Pitfalls to avoid

Excessive nervousness and job-hunting desperation can impede your performance at the application and interview stages, as can sheer exhaustion and dejection at the process of applying and being rejected from role after role. Keeping track of your mindset and re-applying some of the confidence-building frameworks from Chapter One will assist in keeping you on track.

132

Summary

The process of job hunting - and becoming successful at it - was as complicated as it was ever-changing, even before COVID. The combinations and permutations of role, industry, organisation, hiring manager and candidate means there cannot be one quintessential set of advice. Therefore, this chapter has provided a brief outline of this process and has been designed as a springboard to further reading and research that may apply to your job search and may be more current at the time you read this book.

In closing, we would encourage all job seekers to find ways to see the sober task of job hunting in a positive and curious, even playful, light. Some of our favourite stories of successful job hunts have involved candidates attracting the attention of hiring managers with some unorthodox methods. There's the classic story of the man who deduced which route the hiring manager likely took to work each day. He then paid for billboard advertising along this route that promoted his skills and experience. The urban myth tells us that he landed the role, ostensibly for demonstrating initiative.

A current example may involve you investing $50 in a LinkedIn advertising campaign that gets you in front of potential hiring managers. The secret to such tactics is to strike a balance between being creative or edgy and seeming too desperate.

Tools for action

In light of the summary above, we've produced supplementary material that you can access for free of charge, and without the requirement for you to provide your email address, from our website. This material is updated regularly to account for new research and developments.

Please see https://www.careeraftercovid.com/jobhunting for a list of available resources.

134

PART THREE

BEING PART OF
THE WORLD OF
SELF-EMPLOYMENT

CHAPTER TEN

THE ENTREPRENEURIAL DILEMMA

I wanted to live the life; a different life. I didn't want to go to the same place every day and see the same people and do the same job. I wanted interesting challenges.

HARRISON FORD

137

Any time is a good time to start a company.

RON CONWAY

There's no doubt that recessions are a difficult time. However, they also provide unique opportunities for innovative entrepreneurs and start-ups to enter the market. The current economic climate as a result of the pandemic is no different—and if you have an idea for services or goods that can help people adapt to a changing world, there is an opportunity to turn hardship into career and business success.

It's tough to predict in advance the way the business cycle will move. So often the success of a new business relates as much to the personal readiness of the founder or founding team as it does to market conditions. If you feel ready to start your own business in these times, then you should start the preparation process now. That way, as the business cycle picks up, you'll be ready to take advantage of any opportunities as they arise.

Because of the high levels of unemployment for a long time to come, there will be large numbers of applicants for every available job. Why not create your own position rather than wait for other businesses to hire you? You can be part of the economic recovery by building a company that will hopefully last and create employment for other people into the future.

A recession may seem like the perfect time to shelve plans to start a new enterprise. But many top-tier companies took the leap and started up during some significant economic downturns of the past. *Hewlett Packard* and *Hyatt Hotels* did so in the 20th century, and more recently, *Airbnb*, *MailChimp* and *Uber* were founded during recessions, and have gone on to become billion-dollar businesses.

Research from the Bankwest Curtin Economic Centre in 2017 found that Australians who work for themselves or in micro-businesses are more likely to report being very satisfied with their job than those in big companies.[29]

If now seems like the right time for you to explore business ownership, you should research your options thoroughly, and find out if it's going to be the right decision for you. You may never get this much time and space to plan and develop your ideas again.

Is running your own business the way forward?

This chapter is about the personal assessment and the thinking process involved to decide whether you're the right fit to run a business of your own. Since becoming unemployed, Kym and I have gone through this process ourselves. The development of the podcast and the writing of this book have become the seeds of a new enterprise.

The job market is very uncertain at the moment, and even the jobs that are available are seeing thousands upon

---

[29] Cassells, R 2017, 'Happy workers: how satisfied are Australians at work?', Curtin Business School and mwah. Making Work Absolutely Human, Perth, viewed 15 Sep 2020, <http://bcec.edu.au/publications/happy-workers-how-satisfied-are-australians-at-work/.>

thousands of candidates apply for them, making it very hard to cut through and get a job offer. However, it takes some confidence to consider leaving the employment market and setting up in private enterprise. Before taking the leap, it is vital that you undertake a thorough assessment of your suitability for all of the aspects of running your own business. It takes more than just a good idea to run a successful ongoing business operation.

Kym and I did a thorough assessment of our core and transferable skills so that we understood our suitability for this pathway. It's part of the self-reflection and self-assessment that we talked about in Chapter Two.

140

One of the surprising things that our reading revealed was that numerous highly-successful businesses had been born at times of recession, or as a result of a personal crisis in the founders' lives. Major world events result in humans resetting their perspective. The openness of the community to take in new ideas means that business ideas that may not have been possible in the past have greater feasibility in this current climate.

The new markets emerging are not just in niche product or service categories that have sprung up for acute needs during the pandemic such as face masks or hand sanitiser. Market opportunities are evolving, somewhat ironically, from the limitations that COVID has put on us. Scarcity often sparks creativity—being forced to honestly take stock of the resources you have and open your eyes wider than you may have in the pre-pandemic past.

The concept of scarcity in a workplace setting is one I know well. My first professional marketing role was working for a small, underfunded university that was trying to compete with larger, publicly subsidised institutions. I remember hearing the marketing manager of one of these large universities lamenting the $200,000 cut to their marketing budget and thinking to myself, 'That's more than my entire annual marketing budget!'.

However, the small funding envelope I had to manage in that role honed several essential skills. I learned to negotiate lower prices from suppliers, find innovative and inexpensive ways to get our marketing message out and rely on people's goodwill to help project our stakeholder communications further. My tiny budget was frustrating at times, but in retrospect, it was a gift in terms of my professional development.

Turning periods of adversity into the drive for success is one of human beings' most remarkable abilities. And thus, with COVID, the crisis presents countless opportunities for future achievement.

How can I determine if self-employment is right for me?

This exact question was one that we explored in Episode 17 of the *Career after COVID* podcast because so many aspiring entrepreneurs question their suitability for business life. And while it's important not to get dragged down with imposter syndrome as discussed previously, undertaking this initial assessment can save you from wasting time and effort down the road.

Kym outlined the process she takes to gauge students and professionals' suitability, which is fundamentally an assessment of their entrepreneurial mindset.

Entrepreneurial mindset

One of the primary methods Kym has successfully used to assess aspiring entrepreneurs' suitability is to encourage a design-led thinking process. Design thinking is a contemporary tool that supports big-picture conceptualisation, by forcing participants to think beyond their business idea to a larger opportunity space, that may include more or better business opportunities.

Many entrepreneurs start with a well-formed or fixed idea on the product or service offering that they wish to build their business around. The design thinking process asks participants to let go of any attachment to this product idea so that a full exploration of opportunities can occur.

The example that Kym gave in the podcast was of a student who was planning to build an app that enabled university student subscribers to receive free drinks at registered bars and pubs: on the face of it, an idea worth exploring. The student was tasked with formal market research—actually speaking to students—to confirm that such an app would be appealing to them, but in a way that teased out other potential opportunities within a broader 'student social life' category. Instead of "what do you think about a free drinks app?" the suggested conversation-starter became, "How might we enjoy a good social life as a student on a limited budget?"

Kym's entrepreneurial training group found that up to half of the participants withdrew at this point, often citing their discomfort with the process of speaking with potential customers as the reason. Kym initially assumed that the common factor for the withdrawing participants was their introversion. Later, she was astonished when reviewing participants' responses on the Myers Briggs Type Indicator—most of the dropouts had a preference for extroversion.

This surprising result was cause for further analysis, and what the team found was that the common denominator for these withdrawing participants was that they had a fixed mindset, while the participants who persevered tended to have a growth or learning mindset. A significant proportion of students said they found it unnatural to ask, interrupt or impose on people, for fear of being rejected or told 'no'. They were fearful of being wrong or being seen as being wrong – the students thought that they needed to know already so were not open to learning or growth opportunities.

In Kym's discussion with the remaining participants, she discovered that many were inclined towards introversion, but what kept them going was their commitment to learning and growing, even when it got uncomfortable. These students recognised that the perseverance it takes to ask while facing rejection builds strength and creates the 'muscle memory' required to get better at asking as the stakes get higher.

Time and time again, Kym and her team saw this play out. The team were able to predict greater success for students that exhibited a growth mindset at the time of enrolment into their entrepreneurship program. This critical shift resulted in increased retention and many participant success stories during and beyond their time in the program.

Apart from the ideation process, there are logistical considerations to factor in when planning to start a business. The number one question to ask yourself first is:

Are you prepared to take the risk of not succeeding and losing all the money you have invested?

If the answer to this question is 'yes', then the below follow-up questions can help you to discover if you have what it takes to run a successful business.

- Do you believe you can succeed?
- Do you have relevant knowledge of, or experience in, the industry you're considering targeting with your business?
- Do you derive satisfaction from overcoming challenges, or are you easily overwhelmed by problems?
- Do other people tend to come to you to help them make decisions?
- Do you enjoy competition?
- Do you have the discipline and motivation to keep going when times are challenging?
- Do you like to plan, or do you prefer to let matters evolve on their own?
- Are you able to make quick decisions, often under pressure?
- Are you prepared to work long hours, including weekends?
- Do you have sufficient personal savings or an alternative income to live off during the early stages of your business?
- If you have a spouse or dependants, do they understand that there may be less income and time available to spend with them while you are starting your business? Do they support this?

145

- Are you prepared to develop your skills and knowledge in areas that you will need to run your business successfully?
- Are you prepared to seek out advice and mentoring from business advisers and experts?
- And importantly, do you have the requisite skills?

Take the time to consider these questions carefully and be sure to answer them honestly. If you are unsure, talk to someone—ideally a trusted mentor or friend—who has perhaps started their own business and can provide insight and help you put things in perspective. On top of the skills and attributes uncovered in the questions above, you'll need a good understanding (or willingness to learn or ability to enlist support) of the following core business skills:

- financial management
- marketing
- sales and customer service
- communication and negotiation
- leadership
- project management and planning
- delegation and time management
- problem-solving
- networking.

Once you've completed your personal assessment based on the above, it's time to explore the resources and networks around you to confirm whether a new career as a business

146

owner is achievable. Government-funded small business start-up centres, start-up foundations, other business owners and your network of friends and relatives can all be excellent sources of information about what sort of opportunities are available, and how suitable you might be for them.

Consider undertaking one or more of the online questionnaires that ascertain suitability for self-employment. Other self-awareness exercises related to the identified key attributes above (e.g. growth mindset, leadership, problem-solving, communication, etc.) can provide you with further clues on whether becoming a business owner is a good fit for you. In searching for tests, quizzes and assessments online, stick to those that come from a reputable source and keep an open and flexible mind about the results. Some of the assessments you may have already completed as part of the *tools for action* in previous chapters of this book may also provide helpful information in this regard.

Pitfalls to avoid

There's a litany of common mistakes that people make when they decide that they're ready to establish their own business. Some of the most common include:

- deciding to become self-employed because they dislike their current boss or job

- thinking they have what it takes to be in business because they know their industry extremely well
- assuming that self-employment will automatically result in shorter hours and greater earning capacity
- refusing to get advice or learn from others who have been in business before.

Summary

Considering how self-employment might help you achieve your professional goals and assessing whether business ownership is the right pathway for you is a timely one. Your decision doesn't have to be final, and there will no doubt be some businesses that spring up during the pandemic that are time-limited by the trajectory of COVID. Other people will see the company that they create during these difficult times as something that can become an ongoing 'side hustle' once they return to the employment market.

Furthermore, many people currently out of work are taking the opportunity to set up a business as a way to build their skillset and make them more employable ahead of the return of a buoyant candidate recruitment market.

And finally, if you do decide to pursue self-employment, be sure to maintain your obligations for reporting of job search activity if you're on government benefits.

Tools for action

1) Review your responses to some of the quizzes and tests we have outlined in previous chapters against the key attributes of successful business owners, to see whether you have the aptitude and personality to do well in business.

2) If you haven't already done so, take the time to answer the questions in this chapter, then conduct an honest analysis of what your responses tell you about your suitability to start a business now. If you do identify any gaps, and you are keen to pursue the idea of starting a business, look for learning opportunities to develop your skills in that area.

3) Consider taking one of the online tests that assess your suitability for entrepreneurship. Most of them are not scientifically validated, but they can give you an idea of your strengths and areas for development if you're considering business ownership. The BBC has a quick and helpful one at https://www.bbc.com/news/business-33851439.

We've produced supplementary material that our valued readers can access for free, and without the requirement for an email subscription, from our website. This material is updated regularly to account for new research and developments.

Please see https://www.careeraftercovid.com/selfemployment for a list of available resources.

CHAPTER ELEVEN

TAPPING INTO YOUR GENIUS ZONE

Follow the path of the unsafe, independent thinker. Expose your ideas to the dangers of controversy. Speak your mind and fear less the label of 'crack-pot' than the stigma of conformity. And on issues that seem important to you, stand up and be counted at any cost.

THOMAS J. WATSON

151

Innovation is saying no to a thousand things.

STEVE JOBS

Innovation and the generation of new ideas are at the heart of adapting to changing life or market conditions, whether you're an employee or a business owner.

As human beings, we are naturally inclined to think of ways to solve problems—and right now, innovation and creativity are booming. With COVID changing the way we live and work in a career and business sense, innovative ideas may help you to gain some form of competitive advantage. Finding better ways of working as an employee or building better products and services for your customers can make you more resilient to the economic impacts.

The global indicators of innovative activity often indicate a rise in inventions and idea generation during economic downturns. For example, at the higher end of the innovation spectrum, the United States Patent Office saw an increase in patent filings during and shortly after the Great Recession in 2009 to 2010. [30] When creative people get laid off in the recession, they often turn to inventing solutions and starting businesses that help other people adapt to the new reality, as well as creating a new line of work for themselves.

Your path to success after COVID-19 doesn't have to be an idea worthy of a patent. With careful observation of the people around you, their problems and how they solve them, you could soon have an idea for a rewarding business.

Change and innovation are all around us—but we can tend to focus on the negative impacts of the coronavirus, because

[30] WIPO 2017, *World Intellectual Property Indicators*, report, World Intellectual Property Organization, viewed 15 September 2020, <https://www.wipo.int/edocs/pubdocs/en/intproperty/941/wipo_pub_941_2010.pdf.>

the illness, death rate and drastic economic downturns are the headlines we hear the most.

One of the positive changes that COVID has brought to our working lives is the possibility of breaking down the bureaucracy of many organisations and government departments. Processes that were strictly paper-based and in-person before are now available and accessible online.

A year ago, most companies and government departments would not have countenanced the permission for the great majority of their staff members to work from home. The fear was that productivity would be lost and workers would take advantage of being away from the office unsupervised, with their work left incomplete.

153

A fascinating insight that has come out of the working from home trend during the pandemic is how much time is actually wasted by employees while in the office. The changed mindset of many organisational leaders as a result of this insight is opening up the options for employees to request, and in some cases, demand more flexible working hours and locations.

Some of the other bureaucratic norms and functions that are breaking down include video conferencing instead of flying staff to meetings and the opening up of access to many scientific papers that were hidden behind the paywall of the tightly-controlled and some would say, oligopolistic research journals.

How to encourage innovation and excite your creativity

In times of change, it's important to focus initially on the things that are certain in our lives. As we discussed in Chapter One, it's helpful to recognise the reality of your situation and use that as a grounding (albeit an uncomfortable one) to set yourself up for exploration.

Once you know the reality of your situation, even if it's brutal, you can start to plan your next step forward. Workers who have been laid off, or still employed but thinking of a change, have adjusted their risk appetite due to the pandemic and the ways it has upended our lives. Career or lifestyle options that they would not have considered taking a risk with a year ago now seem possible to at least attempt, because of this greater tolerance for some forms of risk.

In many ways, it's a time of freedom because people are focused on their own survival and not paying attention to the actions of others in a critical way. There's a feeling of kindness, and this creates the chance for ambitious professionals to consider making a change into a new and exciting employment field or business opportunity.

As humans, we are all born with an innate level of creativity, but as we grow older, and begin to fear judgement, we often dampen this creativity and begin to fear change itself. The pandemic does provide an opportunity to reconnect with this side of ourselves, nourish our imagination and generate innovative ideas. The additional time that people have on their hands because of the economic slowdown is a perfect setting to work on our creativity.

It can start with something as simple as making a firm commitment to allowing your creative voice to be heard, and to follow your creative impulses. Without taking away from the spontaneity of your creative journey, a solid plan, with simple steps or a process to anchor your journey through creativity, can end up being a source of comfort, confidence and stability.

If you are undertaking a creative or idea generation process for the first time in your adult life, it's a good idea to consider starting with small steps. Being mindful of your surroundings and observing what is going on around you is a useful way to begin your creative journey. The observation of other humans can help us to devise solutions to their problems, thinking about the pain points, and the challenges that are exercising their minds and hearts.

Creativity takes time and space, so allowing yourself to daydream and meditate is an integral part of the process.

Throughout our journey in recording the *Career after COVID* podcast, Kym and I have, separately and together, taken the time to ideate and daydream about where this year may direct us. The bouncing-around of these ideas between like-minded people has undeniably increased the output of creative thinking and idea generation.

I'm a great believer in following your passions and focusing on reaching your potential as an individual. So many people regret not doing this when they reach the end of their lives. They forge a career and life around an industry or job title that they believe others expected them to undertake.

It's now a common occurrence for workers to be looking for an opportunity to pivot their efforts and move into another part of the economy, or a different way of working. There may not be another more ideal time as this chaotic, disrupted, 'Year of the COVID-19 Pandemic'.

On a practical note, keeping a journal or an ideas notepad can help you to record the problems around you that you see, and that others talk about, which allows you to start to form ideas on how you might solve them. The more you get into the practice of thinking about others' problems and pain points, the more your brain will learn to think of ways to solve even the most basic human issues, like how to cut the middle out of a pineapple.

When talking with others about their pain points or challenges, curiosity is vital. Make sure that you ask all of the critical questions: what, where, when, how, and importantly, why? Reflect on the practical and logical aspects, as well as how this problem affects the person's sense of self and their ego. Critically, observe how and why people around you spend their money to solve a problem in their life and brainstorm other ways to build a business that can get them to part with their hard-earned cash.

Finally, engage with other people, particularly those who are like-minded in terms of innovation and wanting to explore creative problem-solving. Setting up a creative environment and seeking wisdom from others who've gone down this path can help generate ideas, and also provide you with support and confidence to keep going along the way. Critically, your engagement with very 'unlike-minded people'—those who come at life from a completely different perspective, could be the difference between a pedestrian idea and something earth-shattering.

Pitfalls to avoid

Throughout your career, whether it's as an employee, or as an owner of your own business, you're likely to encounter people who are uncomfortable with innovation. For those who are driven by curiosity, this can be difficult to understand, but you may not have a choice other than to find a way to work productively with these people. If innovation, change and growth is part of your organisational goals, part of the role of leaders is bringing team members along the journey of transformation in the most comfortable way possible. One of the reasons that people are uncomfortable with innovation is that they're afraid of the changes that it may bring to their role—change, after all, isn't comfortable. The pandemic has made that abundantly clear to all of us.

However, one of the positives that may come out of the difficult times we are facing is that people's appetite for change and risk-taking will increase. This increase will enable them to better cope with the stress that comes with innovation and growth in their career, or their business lives, in the future.

It can be very threatening and uncomfortable for people who are afraid of these changes, feeling that they are not creative enough and that they would rather be cautious and stick to known ways of working. They may have a naturally pessimistic approach to life and feel that the proposed changes or the new ways of doing things are not going to be effective.

An essential step in understanding these types of non-innovators, especially when you're bursting with ideas, is to get to know other types of personalities. By using a scale such as the Myers Briggs Type Indicator (which we discussed in Chapter Two), you can gain insight into the ways that other personality types approach change and innovation. This insight can assist you in growing and expanding your levels of empathy and enabling you as an employee, a leader or a business owner, to work together for the benefit of the organisation and the individuals involved.

Summary

We've explored the concept of innovation, creativity and idea-generation in the context of COVID-19 and the opportunities to take advantage of, while the global appetite for new ideas, risk and change is in a state of flux. In the following chapters, we'll explore emerging areas of employment and business niches that may become part of your journey of creativity and change after the pandemic.

159

Tools for action

1) Undertake one or more of the innovation or creative skills and attributes assessments. As an example, the **Innovation Traits** test provides valuable insights into four psychometric dimensions to outline the ways you can contribute to innovation in the workplace. Reflect

on the results and how they relate to you both personally and professionally.

2) Undertake some research on business ideas and inventions that have been successful in the past. These ideas may help ignite your thinking in terms of possibilities.

3) Start an ideas notepad or journal where you can record observations of the problems around you that might be solved through innovative thinking.

As with all of our chapters in this book, we've produced supplementary material that you can access for free, and without the requirement for email subscription, from our website. This material is updated regularly to account for new research and developments.

Please see https://www.careeraftercovid.com/ innovation for a list of available resources.

CHAPTER TWELVE

TOP BUSINESS NICHES DURING AND POST-COVID

No niche is too small if it's yours.

SETH GODIN

If you are considering pursuing self-employment as your pathway, it's critical to clearly define your business model, niche and ideal customer from the start.

Why choosing your business niche is critical

In the past, it was usual for businesses to try to market themselves as a one-stop-shop where you could find a range of goods or services to meet a wide assortment of needs. In pre-internet days, this made sense, because it was difficult to access a variety of suppliers outside your local area. But now that we have search engines, things have changed dramatically—and the advent of e-commerce has altered the way that many businesses around the world conduct their commercial operations.

The rise of the internet and online shopping has given businesses the opportunity to source and supply goods and services globally. Similarly, consumers now have the entire worldwide marketplace available to them via their computers. They can select products quickly based on the criteria that are important to them, not just because a product is available in their local area.

As a result, it is no longer as commercially viable to consider being all things to all people. Thus the rise of niche businesses that service a specific group and provide for their needs only. The ability to target consumers across the world means that niche businesses can be substantial and lucrative.

These days, if you go to any e-commerce advisory service or resource, one of the first tasks they will give you is to find your niche—and then, they'll ask you to target a specific slice of your market segment, to increase your chances of success further. Part of the appeal of having a niche business is that you can become a specialist source of knowledge in this area. When this happens, you'll build trust with consumers and can even start to gain notoriety and credibility for that particular type of product or service.

When you achieve this higher level of credibility in the marketplace, you can charge a premium price for your offering. The economics of such a business model with the opportunity to increase your profit margin can enable you to create what is called a lifestyle business. The opportunities to achieve profits without working ridiculous hours each week has become a significant trend. Long before the pandemic, books such as *The 4-Hour Work Week* had popularised this concept and created such an aspiration for many working people.

Niche-based businesses can have further economic advantages. The ability to understand and meet the needs of a small segment of the market means you can spend less money on mass marketing and promotional activities, and be very focused on specific target groups, their behaviours and interests online.

Once you decide that a niche business is for you, the big challenge is, of course, deciding which niche is the right one to pursue.

How to find profitable business niches during COVID

This chapter provides an overview of some of the techniques for assessing the viability of a range of business niche categories. Given the speed of change in markets, up-to-date information is available on the *Career after COVID* website.

A business niche assessment during the pre-pandemic period may have involved a choice between a bricks-and-mortar shopfront and an online shopfront. The speed of adoption of online technologies and platforms during COVID, as well as practical considerations mandated by policies such as lockdown and social distancing, now means that the choice of online business is the only one to take.

The other business model choices involve choosing between:

- selling your invention or creation
- selling something another entity has created
- selling goods or services
- selling physical or virtual/digital products or services.

Fundamentally, your success will come down to the fundamental economic intersection of supply and demand. A lucrative niche is one that is part of a market where there are enough paying customers to ensure a provider can derive an income from servicing them, but not so many other providers servicing them to drive down profit margins.

Products linked to people's hobbies can be profitable niches to target. In my ideation process, I look for markets where there are enthusiasts, as they will often pay a premium. Pet products, devices, homewares and decor, and beauty and skincare products are also popular physical products to target.

Other important considerations with physical products include:

- the weight of the item (and therefore the shipping cost)
- whether there is a fashion or fad element to the product—this can cut both ways, as fad-products can get significant cut-through with marketing channels such as Instagram. The downside is that these markets are fickle and your revenue stream may decline quickly after the trend has passed
- the overall marketability of the product—consideration of whether the design will lend itself to attractive product pictures and exciting videos that can form the basis of a successful content marketing strategy.

As for non-physical products and services, these have also experienced significant growth during the pandemic, as more and more people spend time online. The learning, personal development and coaching niche has seen outstanding growth. It may be worth considering if you have expertise or skills in a particular area that you believe others will be willing to pay to learn. I have heard of dozens of successful businesses that have seen business growth during COVID, across areas like music tuition, baking skills, book authoring, online marketing coaching and art classes, just to name a few.

Keeping an eye on emerging market trends is also advisable. It is possible to access articles online that list these trends. Some of the currently trending ideas that Kym and I discussed in Episode 12 of the podcast include reverse globalisation, an anxious society, e-commerce, e-learning, e-fitness, e-health, cybersecurity, plant-based food and dark kitchens.

Another filter to use when assessing niches is to consider your own interests, passions and values discussed in Section One of this book. Which product or service sector would you be excited to get out of bed and work on every day?

Practical steps to refine your business niche

These are the steps that Kym and I have been following while researching business niches:

1. We read very widely, every publication and subscription we can afford across news, current affairs, and several industry segments in which we have an interest. Importantly, we also read and

observe outside of our comfort zone to understand potential target markets beyond our close circle of friends and contacts. Stories that cover problems or issues people are facing can sometimes form the basis of a problem-solving business idea—whether it's helping them make money, entertaining them to cure boredom or helping them feel better about themselves.

2. We keep an ideas journal—in my case, the Evernote app on my phone so I can always access it. I save articles, write notes and also record my voice to talk about something if I need my hands free when an idea pops into my head.

3. We write down all of our ideas using the template available at careeraftercovid.com/tools that helps classify them into broad categories.

4. Our next step is rating each idea according to the criteria in the template—which problem(s) it solves, the demand for the product or service, levels of competition, whether it's trendy or evergreen—using a range of research tools outlined with the template.

167

Pitfalls to avoid

In finding the right niche to target with your business idea, it's essential to be clear on what a niche really is. I work from the definition of a niche as a group of similar people with a shared problem, passion or interest. Many business owners decide to create a niche business around a particular product. Still, the rate of change in technology and consumer interests may mean their product-based niche quickly becomes out of date and irrelevant. Focusing on solving a problem is a significant factor in having a long-lasting successful niche business.

Like so many pitfalls that we mention in this book, failing to do adequate research, analysis, and preparation is also a common issue when deciding on a niche. Spend sufficient time gathering the best information you can on market demand, profitability and future growth to help make an informed decision about your business idea.

Summary

This chapter provided an overview of our tried and tested ways to find and monetise business niche areas. A critical factor in the exploration of business ideas is to focus on people's problems and how you might solve them, rather than a product or service that is not flexible to change.

In the coming chapters, we'll provide current advice on the steps you'll need to take to get your business off the ground.

Tools for action

1) Research is critical to ensure you choose a niche that will be successful, meaningful or profitable, depending upon your objectives and values. You can search the internet for ideas and make a list of the possibilities that appeal to you.

2) The other essential step is validation. Online tools such as Google Trends can give you data on whether your niche idea is popular or growing. At a more advanced level, search engine and keyword tools such as ahrefs.com and SEMrush.com provide detailed data on which subjects are being searched worldwide and form a valuable part of your idea validation.

As with all of our chapters in this book, we've produced supplementary material that you can access for free, and without the requirement for an email subscription from our website. This material is updated regularly to account for new research and developments.

Please see https://www.careeraftercovid.com/businessniche for a list of available resources.

CHAPTER THIRTEEN

5,4,3,2,1 – IT'S TIME TO LAUNCH

The way to get started is to quit talking and start doing.

WALT DISNEY

If you're ready to embark on the journey to entrepreneurship and business ownership, this chapter, and the ones following, will provide you with the steps to ensure you're well-prepared and that your business has the best chance of success.

Part of the preparation for success is awareness of and learning from the pitfalls and failure points of other businesses, so we have included information on potential blind spots in your preparation for launch.

Why the launch phase
of your business is critical

A thorough planning process is an essential first step for your new business. It allows you to test the feasibility of your idea and is a must-have if you're planning on securing external funding or investment. It also provides the basis for an ongoing guide to operations, which will give you a solid foundation and assist you in moving forward as the business grows.

Before the pandemic hit, Australia had more than two million small businesses in operation[31]. Challenges brought on by changing retail models plus the drying up of business finance after the Banking Royal Commission meant many small companies were already on shaky ground. Only time will tell the number of businesses that don't make it through the pandemic, even with Government support.

According to a 2018 study by business advisory group HLB Mann, a staggering four in five Australian businesses do not have a working business plan in place, undermining their ability to resolve problems and maintain a steady growth trajectory.

[31] Australian Small Business and Family Enterprise Ombudsman 2019, Small Business Counts, report, viewed 11 September 2020, <https://www.asbfeo.gov.au/sites/default/files/documents/ASBFEO-small-business-counts2019.pdf.>

The ultimate reasons that lead to business failure

It is critical to be aware of the conditions that can lead to business failure by avoiding common pitfalls. A study conducted in 2015 by the University of Technology, Sydney, outlined reasons (in order of frequency) that can lead to the collapse of a private enterprise undertaking.

1. Inefficient handling of funds and cash flow
2. Poor overall management
3. Negligent conduct towards record-keeping
4. Sales and marketing issues
5. Poor staff management
6. Inability to accept and act on external advice
7. General economic circumstances
8. Personal problems

173

Being mindful about the factors as mentioned earlier allows you to appraise your current business strategy critically. Financial management is deemed to be the most significant contributing aspect to efficient business administration. Failure to successfully handle available funds is attributed to be responsible for 32% of potential business failures.

Financial mismanagement can result from:

- a substandard or inaccessible location
- failure to cater to customer's needs and wants
- deferred invoicing and unfavourable prices
- delayed payments and excess credit issuance

- inventory issues—dead stock and shortfalls
- absence of sufficient staff for customer service
- inability to service debt or chase up outstanding invoices
- supplier infidelity and unavailability of necessary raw materials
- lack of promotion, marketing and advertisement
- absence of quality workmanship
- lacking information regarding product and market forces
- ineffective cash control and swindling of goods or cash

Typically, a mixture of multiple factors piles up and results in the downfall of the business in question. Therefore, an entrepreneur must pursue an approach that includes careful analysis of all the working parts in the enterprise and superior management to avoid a business collapse.

What is a business plan?

A well-written business plan can take one of many forms. A typical business plan technique sets the vision and direction of your business. It assesses the viability of the idea using a tool such as a SWOT (Strengths, Weaknesses, Opportunities, Threats) analysis.

In the early years of the 21st Century, more and more entrepreneurs have started planning their businesses and verifying their business ideas using modern 'canvas' planning tools. A Lean Canvas approach is another way to plan your business and refine its vision and your offering. Kym and I discussed this approach in Episode 18 of the *Career after COVID* Podcast.

Lean Canvas is an adaptation of the Business Model Canvas by Alexander Osterwalder, which Ash Maurya created in the spirit of the Lean Start-up (fast, concise and effective)[32]. Lean Canvas promises an actionable and entrepreneur-focused business plan on one page. It focuses on problems, solutions, key metrics and competitive advantages and can be completed (in fact, should be completed) in twenty minutes or less.

How to plan for business launch using Lean Canvas

These are the steps that Kym advises business start-ups to follow when preparing plans for business launch:

---

[32] Maurya, A 2012, *Running Lean*, Second Edition, O'Reilly, Sebastopol.

Validate your ideas and build your formal business plan

The Lean Canvas allows you to either plan for a new business, or to reassess your current business to see how to reorient your offering or approach to current market conditions. It's a quick and powerful way to define and validate your business idea—and if it takes more than twenty minutes to fill in, you are doing it wrong.

The process of completing the Lean Canvas and continually referring to it builds your mindset so that you are always focusing on your customer and their pain points, testing assumptions and updating the canvas as necessary.

It consists of nine boxes on one page with each box containing space for a few dot-point answers. The questions are explored below.

The Lean Canvas template

1a. Who is my customer?

1b. Who are the early adopters in my customer group, with the most urgent need to resolve their pain point?

Answering the above questions forces you to take the time to understand your customer base as profoundly as possible.

2a. What are my customers' pain points and problems that need solving?

2b. What are the existing solutions to these problems?

3. What are my proposed solutions to these problems?

The above questions put the focus on problems and solutions.

4. What are the fixed and variable costs of providing a solution to the problems (including costing for your own time)?

5. Where will the revenue come from?

Straight away, you get a sense of the cash flow equation for your proposed business, and whether it is likely to be positive or negative.

6. What is my business' unfair advantage? It could be a patent you own from an invention, or in the case of a service business, it may be your personal brand.

Think about what your business will have that others will find difficult to replicate.

7. What is your unique selling proposition (which may become your business tagline)?

It's best to keep this sharp and succinct; aim to write one sentence.

8. How will I reach my customers, through either inbound or outbound channels?

This box gets you thinking about potential channels to market.

9. What are the key metrics to tell me where my business is at?

And finally, how will you know how well your business is doing?

Whichever approach you decide on for the full business plan, we highly recommend that the process finishes with the preparation of one-page current action plan.

The process of business planning

When starting a company, you'll need a business model to work with. It will revolve around the way your business adds value (and profits from doing so). There are several steps involved with business planning, none of which need to be overcomplicated.

Fundamentally, there are four things that all businesses do:

- Create things—this may come in the form of a product or service. You'll also need to determine which markets are worth entering and how you can contribute to them.
- Market things—whatever the company provides, people won't buy it if they have no awareness of it.

It also won't sell if people can't wrap their heads around it or get motivated enough to purchase it.
- Deliver things—it doesn't matter if your offering is a service or product, you must deliver the things you promise to.
- Count things—many people would refer to this as 'finance', but it also entails analysing and measuring data that is intangible *and* tangible.

Some of the significant business models worth considering include:

1. Service/product—companies can develop their own services or products and sell them. This tends to be the most popular approach. Your branded offering will be distributed through an assortment of channels before being delivered either digitally or tangibly. The service/product might be part of either an ongoing subscription or a one-time purchase for customers.

2. Reseller—a reseller doesn't necessarily warehouse or produce the things they sell. Instead, they find various products or represent certain brands.

The profit resellers make is the difference between the cost to acquire a product and the resale price. Affiliate marketers can be classified as resellers, as can VARs (Value Added Resellers) and physical retail stores.

3. Broker—a broker profits from transaction fees involved in the exchange of goods and services. There has been an explosion in this category, thanks to the influx of broker platforms on the internet. Brokers bring sellers and buyers together to finalise a transaction, no matter where they are. This particular business model involves marketplace creation, transaction handling, and security optimisation.

4. Aggregator—aggregators build communities, then charge fees for people to access those communities. In several ways, news sites and publications fit this business model perfectly. They build subscriber bases before allowing advertisers to promote things to the community (usually via positioned ads).

Those who have a business idea should consider the following key points.

Market potential. Establish if a market exists for your potential idea, and, if so, find out how big it is. There isn't anything wrong with focusing on a specific niche; however, you won't achieve any success if no demand exists for your offering.

Ideal customer. Define the qualities and characteristics of customers that you plan on serving. By doing so, you'll get a sense of the market's size, as well as how to target it.

Competitive landscape. Determine what kind of competition you're going up against to feel out the types of value propositions they have.

Value proposition. Why should somebody choose you over a competitor? All entrepreneurs are proud of their concepts, but if they can't easily explain what makes it worth buying, success will never come.

Distribution channels. Your service, product, or idea can be marketed in all sorts of ways. You can use marketplaces, sales reps, retail stores, e-commerce sites, distributors, and direct sales forces (or a mix of these options). Expenses and profits associated with each option can differ based on the business model used.

181

Revenue streams. There needs to be a primary source of revenue generation. With that said, the strongest business models are the ones that factor in other ways of bringing in revenue and adding value. For example, consultants may publish advertisements on their blogs, sell books and promote book speaking engagements as secondary sources of income, the primary one being the actual consultations.

Strategic relationships. Develop a partnership with organisations that have services or products relevant to your business model. For example, software companies might have relationships with program developers, and their collaboration improves a product.

When determining which business model to use, it is worth knowing how traditional models operated. Learning from the successes and mistakes of others can teach you what you should and shouldn't be doing.

Whichever business model you end up proceeding with, we encourage you to finish the process by preparing an action plan (ideally on a single page). This business planning step will give you a sense of how things stand now and how you want them to go. You'll be able to implement solutions at suitable times while you move towards bringing your vision to fruition. Chronicling the results of the business planning process will also go a long way.

Your action plan should, at a minimum, contain the following:

- 'Now' analyses: a summary of your existing situation. You'll have the ability to fit as many as five points here. Which of them describe your issues accurately at the moment?
- 'Where' analyses: describe what you envisioned. What type of competitive advantage do you have? What about critical objectives? These elements should be summarised here.
- Strategies: what key strategies will you perfect over the year? Write down at least three or four.
- Action plans: write down the steps to take here. You don't have to write down every step involved in

your action plan—just the important ones for your strategy and how the delivery of the key objectives will be measured.

- Timing: when do you intend to accomplish your results? List your results in a prioritised order. Make notes that illustrate who is specifically accountable.

Assessing numerous business ideas

Entrepreneurs sometimes have a large number of ideas and are unable to decide which one to pursue. Certain criteria can help narrow down ideas. Do your ideas correspond with your experience, passion, and skills? Will your idea help you accomplish your overall goals?

A method that Kym and I use to hone in on a business niche idea is to ask a trusted mentor to name three business categories or niches from which we must choose one. By limiting the choice, it forces us to focus on the options, and importantly, to form resistance to some or all of the three choices, thereby revealing what we **really** want to engage in. For example, I told Kym she had to choose between cars, planes and motorbikes – all forms of transport. She didn't much like the sound of any of them, and this pushed her back to her real passion: horse riding.

Business name brainstorming

After validating and confirming your idea's feasibility, you can set up a business entity. Brainstorm some names and check to see if they aren't taken already. You should also find out if a domain name for your business' name is available. If they are, you can buy both your domain and business name trademarks.

Choosing a business structure

You'll need to make decisions about a business' structure when you launch one. The type of structure you choose will be contingent on what your business does, how big it is, and the way it will be run. You will need to consider things like taxes, asset protection, set-up costs, and more. Do your due diligence and get professional advice if you have uncertainties about anything.

Four common business structure types exist in Australia:

- Sole trader—the most basic structure, in which you will have complete control.
- Partnership—at least two people will distribute losses or income.
- Incorporation—the structure is more complex; however, it places limits on liabilities, because corporations are seen as separate legal entities from the individuals involved.
- Trust—the trustee will be responsible for a company's operations.

It is worthwhile to get professional advice about which structures will best accommodate your needs. If you plan on conducting business with another company, be sure to chronicle this arrangement. The obligations and rights of all involved parties should be documented. That way, you'll be able to resolve disputes that come up between owners.

Shareholder agreements and partnership agreements are the most common ways of documenting a business relationship's structure. Each party involved should have a lawyer draft and customise the relevant documents.

Determining legal obligations

There may be certain regulations and laws that dictate the way your business is run, depending on what it does. It pays to read up on these legalities. Find out if you are expected to hold certain permits or licenses. Perhaps an employee needs to have a certain skill level to perform at your place of business. Maybe there are rules about refunds in your region?

It's also imperative to think about how your business' intangible assets will be protected, especially your intellectual property (IP). Your IP may be comprised of assets like copyrights, trademarks, domain names and branding. It might even involve unique concepts or formulas. Company owners can often underestimate how valuable an intellectual property can be, so it is advisable to seek professional advice from an IP legal professional.

Other ways of protecting yourself involve drafting conditions and terms properly. This will be especially for payment terms, as all company owners must be compensated at some point.

A privacy policy should also be written to keep your company compliant with all privacy legislation. A privacy policy also tells customers that the personal information they provide you with will be handled professionally and responsibly.

Employing and team-building

Legal obligations that you have will increase the more your business grows – particularly after you start employing staff and contractors. You will have to think about employment conditions if you plan on hiring employees. What will you offer staff if you do? There are minimum standards set in Australia, which apply to every employee (for example, minimum wage). Further, certain industries offer rewards to employees as a kind of 'safety net'.

Familiarise yourself with such standards. The obligations you have as part of the *Occupational Health & Safety Act* and *Fair Work Act* must be determined to ensure that you are lawfully operating your company.

You are encouraged to draft a formal employment arrangement with employees. This will document the obligations and rights that each party involved has. It will also address particulars in the event that a dispute between you and an employee arises.

Understanding your finances and creating a budget

A budget assists business owners to track their business' financial health. It will help you direct money to the places it is most needed, hopefully for the best return on investment. Budgets coordinate your spending habits and income, as well as help you to allocate finances for various activities and items.

A budget can also help you establish business objectives, make wiser choices, and receive financing if needed.

There are three steps to take when putting together a budget for your business.

1. **Creating a budget.** If you are just starting out, there are several things that you will need to factor in when putting a budget together. Some of them include expected income, timeframe, and calculation of variable and fixed costs.

2. **Monitoring your budget.** A fundamental bookkeeping system will be needed to track finances. You need to make sure your expenditures stay within the boundaries of your budget.

3. **Using your budget.** A budget analysis helps you make smarter business decisions. It will stop you from spending more money than you should, as well as show you how to reduce costs. You'll be

able to stop purchasing things that aren't helping your business bring in income. If extra funds are available, allocate them towards debt as best you can. A monetary safety net should be created to cover unexpected events. Ultimately, though, the purpose of a budget is to facilitate business growth and keep your expenses in check.

Prepare your marketing plan for launch

The following are some of the key steps to prepare for the actual market launch for your business:

- ensure you have a reliable source of inventory
- choose and set up social media accounts
- create a logo and print stationery and marketing materials if required
- set up a website and extend functionality as required
- set up an email helpdesk to streamline customer service
- create hype and anticipation before launch.

Pitfalls to avoid

As mentioned earlier in the chapter, there are many reasons that businesses can fail, even in the first few months when founders' energy and enthusiasm levels are high. Here are some of the pitfalls to watch out for:

- lack of cash flow
- unrealistic financial projections
- not defining the target audience
- over-hype
- poor market research
- no focus on your competition
- not addressing your weaknesses
- not knowing your distribution channels
- being inconsistent
- not having a marketing plan
- impatience
- overspending
- under-pricing your product or service
- not forming the right business entity
- thinking you don't need insurance
- not having a written agreement with your business partners and/or staff
- waiting too long to hire or constructing the wrong team
- not having a website
- waiting too long to seek financing.

189

Summary

We've provided a step-by-step action plan for the process of planning your business, ascertaining the feasibility of your product or service idea and preparing for the launch to market. In the next chapter, we will provide an overview of the key strategies for business growth in the time of the COVID-19 pandemic.

Tools for action

1) Small business support organisations provide detailed information on business set-up, well beyond the brief explanation we have provided here. Find your local government business centre and make use of their resources, events and services to prepare for a successful launch.

As with all of our chapters in this book, we've produced supplementary material that you can access for free from our website. This material is updated regularly to account for new research and developments, but it should not be taken as professional financial advice. Readers are advised to seek their own professional advice with respect to legal and financial decisions.

Please see https://www.careeraftercovid.com/ businesslaunch for a list of available resources. Readers of our book can use the link above without needing to provide an email address for subscription.

CHAPTER FOURTEEN

SEIZE THE OPPORTUNITIES

And the day came when the risk to remain tight in a bud was more painful than the risk it took to blossom.

ANAÏS NIN

191

Once your business is established (or if your business is already up and running) you can start preparing for growth. Even if you don't want to make your business more of a management challenge than it already is, business owners can find ways to continue expanding their reach to make up for any attrition in their customer base. As the saying goes, 'If you're not growing, your business is in decline'.

Kym and I explored the concept of business growth in the *Career after COVID* podcast, Episode 19, and devised some strategies and tactics for business owners to apply to help their business to survive and hopefully thrive during and beyond the pandemic.

Why it's important to scale your business now

For many business owners, the current economic climate does not seem the time to be planning for growth, so the idea of scaling up now may be surprising. Indeed, consumer spending is depressed in most markets around the world—and in specific industries such as hospitality or tourism that are severely affected by lockdowns, the bottom line is survival rather than plans for growth. However, it is important we are realistic about our unique business circumstances and options.

Firstly, consider the investment that you've made in setting your business up—everything from your business name registration, your domain name and getting your website up and running. You may also have stock on hand and a big email list of previous customers and prospects. Plus, maybe you've invested in marketing materials and have been developing your product or service offering. In these circumstances, it's a tough decision to walk away. Some businesses will only have the option to close, and that's a regrettable loss, not only to those people and their families, but also to our economy in a larger sense. Our hearts genuinely go out to those people, just like we feel for those who have lost paid employment as a result of the COVID crisis.

Others will find a way to pivot and introduce other products or services that will help their business stay afloat. Some parts of the economy are ripe for growth. And whether that involves growing what you are already doing or changing things up and going into a related market space, there are options to consider.

One of the key aspects of business that most business owners will have explored already is an online offering. For instance, there have been many good news stories of fitness studios, Pilates or yoga classes, kid's karate classes and music classes all being offered online, enabling customers to continue their learning or fitness journey and the business owner to keep a revenue stream during the pandemic.

Another business I know of produces skincare products for babies and children. At first, the owners were unsure of where to direct their efforts once the pandemic began and sales slowed down. They then decided to focus on hand sanitiser which was in short supply due to panic buying. Within their skincare business they already had well-established supply networks, which meant they could get their hand sanitiser product to market quickly, and they replaced the lost income from their other product lines with this new, high-demand product line.

Fashion businesses throughout the world are another great example of this type of agility, with many adding face protection masks to their product range. This ability to think creatively about your offerings and replace lost

193

income from one part of the business with a new line, plays a big part in keeping the business afloat.

Another reason to take steps to grow your business now is longevity in the competitive landscape. If your competitors are closing up their shops, and you can somehow find a way to survive, then you could well be the last business standing when the economy recovers, and be ready to capitalise on people's new spending habits.

How to grow your business

Fundamentally, there are just three main ways to grow your business:

1. Increase the number of customers
2. Increase the average order value of customers
3. Increase the number of times customers return and buy again.

Each action listed below is designed to address one or more of these fundamental growth strategies. They are tactics that Kym and I have applied in the businesses that we have set up and run in the past, as well as new ideas, generated from working with clients in the small business space. Depending upon your cost of acquisition and your profit margin, it may be more profitable to focus your efforts on increasing repeat purchasing or the average amount a customer spends when they buy from you.

Get to know your customers better

You may feel that you know your customers very well, but since the whole world has changed, it's an ideal time to engage with them more intensely and really take the time to understand what the major pain points are for them right now. Business and consumer confidence surveys can provide some general idea of customer sentiment, but there's nothing more powerful than speaking directly with your own customers. You may find that your customers will give you new ideas on how to provide more value for them. At the very least you will forge a stronger relationship and help prevent customer attrition.

195

The concept of customer lifecycle can be useful in this context. Understanding how you acquire customers through initial marketing efforts, how much each customer spends, how often they purchase, and whether there are additional offerings you can provide to increase sales value are all important insights to assist in growing your revenue and profit.

Be mindful and transparent in your communication

When it comes to customer and stakeholder communication, it's a good idea to be conscious of what might be going on for your customers, and ensure your communications are sensitive and helpful rather than trying to be clever by making light of the situation.

The focus has to be on meeting customers' needs, rather than communicating in a way that implies you may be trying to profit from the pandemic. Be sensitive to everyone, as you never know who is really suffering—whether they've lost their job, been sick, had someone close to them get ill or pass away of COVID, or been locked down and are suffering mental health issues as a result.

We have also seen the importance of communicating transparently and honestly about how COVID is affecting your business and your service delivery to customers. Examples of this include changes to store opening times (update this on your Google Business listing as well as your website) and making customers aware of increased product shipping times.

Put customers first

Depending upon your business niche, an excellent customer service process will ensure you stand out from your competitors and grow your revenue and profits. Online reviews on Google Maps, Facebook, Trip Advisor and Yelp are so incredibly critical these days—any business who owner ignores customer service does so at their peril!

A customer service plan, supplemented by a training program for staff, is a vital ingredient in ensuring your staff members know what is expected of them and how to delight customers to ensure repeat business and good reviews.

Similarly, the establishment of a loyalty program, where regular customers can earn rewards for choosing to buy from your business, can also drive growth in repeat business, revenue and profit. Offering incentives for current customers to refer their network to your business is another way to grow your customer base.

Focus on improving value for money

The changes in working practices and lifestyle during the pandemic presents an excellent opportunity to reassess your customers' perception of the value your products or services provide, relative to your competitors. An aspect of your service that customers never saw as worthwhile may figure highly in their list of desirable service attributes, and may present an opportunity for an additional income stream, or a replacement for an income stream that has disappeared due to the pandemic.

Keeping the lines of communication with your customers open and taking the time to integrate feedback into your offerings and overall business strategy could reap revenue dividends for you even in this difficult economic period.

Understand your competitors

Part of the business growth equation is reducing or preventing customer attrition to competitor businesses.

197

Knowing who your competitors are and having an insight into their strategies and activities is a key component of market research. It's something that should be built into ongoing market sensing, as things can change quickly, especially in the marketplace that has been turned upside down by COVID.

The competitive landscape for your business today might look altogether different in a year, or even six months' time. If your competitors are as ambitious as you, it's possible they could be planning to launch a multitude of new products or diversify into new markets. One of the ways I keep across my competition is to sign up for job alerts in my industry. The positions that your competitors are hiring for can provide clues as to their future growth strategy. Patent applications, their marketing communications activities and their strategic partnerships can also provide insight.

Move online where you can and find ways to automate

With a global increase in online activity, it's so important to present your business well online, not just in terms of an attractive interface and product pictures, but really thinking about offering additional value through online channels. On Episode 20 of the podcast, we provided the example of the local mechanic who created video resources for his customer base during lockdown—simple things like changing motor oil and changing a tyre. Your first response might be to think the mechanic will lose business as a

198

result of people doing it themselves, but it actually grew loyalty amongst his customer base. And after lockdown lifted, he has been busier than ever.

Online booking systems have also boomed during the pandemic, cutting phone and email time for administrative staff manually booking appointments. Any way you can find to make your business run smoother can assist in providing higher standards of customer service and potentially cutting costs.

Events, social media and other marketing outreach

It goes without saying that your business' marketing and communications strategy should be guided by your overall business growth objectives. Within the limits of your business budget, it's still a good idea to continue investment in your external outreach and marketing.

Continuing to update your business' social media profiles, running events, either in-person or online, depending upon your audience and location, is still paying dividends for businesses that can find ways to meet their customers' needs.

Staying top of mind in your industry is also still important, by attending events to build your own network, even if they are virtual events.

Continuous focus on your sales funnel is also critical. Once someone sees your advertisement or organic (unpaid) online content, it's important to consider how the relationship gets nurtured so that they eventually become your customer. Your current customer base is your most likely source of new business, either through repeat purchases or referrals, so focus effort on keeping in touch with them through email marketing and regular updates on your social media pages. A special offer for these loyal customers can provide an instant lift to sales volumes and get your offering back at the top of their minds.

Give back to the community

Community sponsorship is another marketing tool that can go a long way in these times. There's a lot of community organisations, such as sporting clubs who have been doing it tough. If there's some way that you can help them out and get some advertising or profile-raising opportunities as a result of that, it can be a great way to grow a loyal customer base and support your local community.

Pitfalls to avoid

A period of rapid business growth is a time for additional vigilance. Businesses failing because they grew too rapidly is a reasonably common occurrence, and in podcast Episode 20, we discussed the importance of immediate, medium and long-term goals that are measurable against pre-agreed metrics.

Planning in stages allows the building of confidence as your business grows. Promising to customers and stakeholders only what you are certain you can deliver is an absolute must. Risk-taking is the essence of enterprise, but it must always be within a framework of calculated risk.

Summary

Business growth may appear to be wishful thinking during these chaotic times and economic uncertainty, but we all know of businesses that have grown and thrived since COVID hit and where possible, we should aim to be part of the good-news story of business success.

In this chapter, we have listed some of the key strategies and tactics you can consider deploying to increase your customer base, revenue and hopefully sustainable, meaningful business growth and scale during and after the pandemic.

Tools for action

There are literally millions of web sites and pages, podcast episodes, books and online courses dedicated to helping business owners meet their growth objectives. Some of our favourites have been referenced throughout these last few chapters. For the sake of completeness, here they are again, along with others (in no particular order):

Books

- *Good to Great* by Jim Collins
- *The 4-Hour Work Week* by Timothy Ferriss
- *The 7 Habits of Highly Effective People* by Stephen R. Covey
- *Atomic Habits* by James Clear

Podcasts

- *Niche Pursuits* with Spencer Haw
- *Online Marketing Made Easy* with Amy Porterfield
- *Smart Passive Income* with Pat Flynn
- *Social Media Marketing* with Michael Stelzner

As with all of our chapters in this book, we've produced supplementary material that you can access for free from our website. This material is updated regularly to account for new research and developments.

Please see https://www.careeraftercovid.com/businessgrowth for a list of available resources. Readers of our book can use the link above without needing to provide an email address for subscription.

WHAT TO DO WHEN SOMEONE CLOSE TO YOU LOSES THEIR JOB

With the pandemic causing economic downturn and mass job losses across the world, it's likely that you will know someone who has been, or soon will be, laid off. If you're wondering how to assist, we've gathered our best ideas based on our own situation when our jobs ended in March 2020.

To begin with, some of the tips we outlined in Chapter One ring true when supporting others who have lost their jobs. Acknowledging the loss, celebrating the transition, helping the person to be kind to themselves by separating the job from their own sense of self, and gently discouraging blame or vengeful thoughts are good places to start.

If the person is not in financial difficulty, then a care package of the little things that they might not buy for themselves - flowers, chocolates, a gift voucher for one of the video

205

or music streaming services – is a thoughtful gift that says "I value you" rather than "I pity you."

Welfare check

An important first step is to ensure that the recently laid-off person is in a safe environment and has their basic needs catered for. Depending on how close your relationship is with this person, consider enquiring about their access to these basic needs and whether you can provide (or refer to a service provider offering) one or more of the following:

- regular, nutritious meals
- temporary and long-term accommodation
- unemployment benefits
- relief with utility bills
- clothing
- money or gift vouchers for incidental expenses
- professional healthcare and mental health support

The Australian Department of Social Services maintains a list of emergency relief services, available from their website at dss.gov.au. If you are in a position to do so, please encourage the unemployed person to get in contact with support services as early as possible so that the situation does not escalate. This is especially true concerning housing and accommodation, where waiting lists for emergency or temporary accommodation can be lengthy.

Job-search assistance

Offering to assist with a friend's job search is a kind gesture, but one that can be fraught with awkwardness if not approached sensitively. An open-ended question or statement such as one of the following can be a kind gesture that is not loaded with inferences of failure or pessimism:

- "Can I help you with anything related to your job search?"
- "Can I put you in touch with someone from my network that can assist?"
- "Let me know if you need someone to proofread your CV or cover letters when you're applying for jobs."

In addition, offering your home office resources to enable your friend to prepare job applications (if they've lost access to their work computer and printer), an outfit from your wardrobe for job interviews or, if the job-seeker has children, a few hours of babysitting, would be likely to be well-received assistance with no cash outlay to make it awkward.

LinkedIn assistance

The single, most-helpful action my former colleagues and friends took when I lost my job was to endorse my LinkedIn skills or write an unsolicited LinkedIn recommendation based on our experience of working together. It is such a concrete, public way to offer job-hunting support and was very touching to receive these endorsements (which I could choose to display on my profile - or not) at a stressful time.

Summary

Checking in with those who you care about has been a vital source of connection for everyone throughout this pandemic. Our unemployed friends and family members may be even more overwhelmed than others, and in need of extra levels of care, communication and assistance.

Avoid contributing to the overwhelm by communicating that you are available to chat with when they need it, and agree to only check-in with them at certain intervals (such as once or twice a week).

208

Tools for action

We've created a day-to-day guide for the unemployed to assist with the first month after they lose their job, providing some structure when it can seem overwhelming. It covers such things as:

- Registering for unemployment benefits, welfare, emergency support and Government job-seeking assistance
- Self-care and positive mindset development
- Ensuring your contact details can be found by employers
- Updating your CV
- Developing a new skill
- Volunteer work
- Networking and professional associations
- Identifying and researching potential employers
- Applying and interviewing for jobs
- Job application follow-up

The full guide is available at careeraftercovid. com/daybyday

AFTERWORD

Dear Reader,

Thank you for joining us on this journey through unemployment and hopefully onto meaningful and satisfying paid employment.

As we send this book off to be published, in the last quarter of 2020, some parts of our lives have reverted to near-normal. However, the uncertainty of the virus' trajectory remains a constant in our existence, and that of many around the world.

Our hope is that our stories and the actionable advice we have included here have equipped you with the tools you need to move into a successful post-COVID life. As we said at the beginning, we are fundamentally optimistic about the strength of the human spirit and that the crises reverberating around the world provide the impetus for us, as a race, to come out the other side in a better place.

For us, the authors, we are fortunate to have reached a better place. We could not suppress our entrepreneurial urges and are starting 2021 with our business ideas getting off the ground.

We would love to hear your stories – please reach out from our website at careeraftercovid.com or follow us and tell us your stories on our social media pages:

Facebook.com/careeraftercovid
Instagram.com/careeraftercovid
linkedin.com/company/career-after-covid-19
twitter.com/careerrockstars

And if you enjoyed this book, we'd be grateful for a review on your favourite book retailer's site, on our Facebook page or on Google.

Thanks again for your support. We appreciate you.

Fleur Hull and Kym Kraljevic
#careeraftercovid

ABOUT
THE AUTHORS

Career after COVID is a collaboration between career strategist and marketer, Fleur Hull, and entrepreneurship strategist, Kym Kraljevic.

Fleur Hull

Fleur is a high-energy and results-driven career coach with a passion for personal and organisational growth. She thrives in high-pressure business situations and feels most fulfilled when she has played a role in assisting people and organisations to reach their potential. Her greatest strengths are in bringing people and information together to maximise opportunity and success for all.

Throughout her younger years, Fleur's parents ran numerous successful small businesses, and she absorbed the imperatives of operational and people management through many dinnertime conversations as well as part-time work in family business ventures. These businesses ranged from garden centres, a pickle factory, a spice packing business, store protection services, ergonomic furniture sales and office design and fit-out services.

After graduating in economics and Japanese, Fleur worked in a Japanese local government office and honed her understanding of Japanese language and culture. Her passion for lifelong learning saw Fleur go on to complete two master's degrees in marketing and education management.

The bulk of Fleur's professional experience is in the higher education sector, for the first seven years in marketing, communications and student support at a young university, whose enrolments grew nearly three-fold during her four years in charge of student recruitment. She presented to and advised thousands of high school and mature-age students about their career and course choices during this time. This ignited Fleur's passion for seeing people find a satisfying and rewarding path through their lives.

Fleur then leveraged this experience, as well as the knowledge gained from two degrees, to position herself as a senior strategy and change adviser in the education sector. Her management roles gave her inside perspective on the hiring process, and what makes a candidate attractive to an employer. Fleur has personally reviewed thousands of job applications and resumes for more than 100 roles in her career journey, positioning her as a valued adviser to anyone seeking a job.

After a major client ended her consulting contract as a result of COVID-19 in March 2020, Fleur and her former colleague, Kym Kraljevic, decided to start a podcast about the impact of the pandemic on employment and the economy. With more than twenty episodes now published, and growing numbers of downloads, Fleur and Kym decided to write this book to provide an up-to-date set of tools for early and mid-career professionals and paraprofessionals to find an employment pathway in life that is fulfilling, rewarding and hopefully contributes to national economic recovery.

Fleur's background in economics and marketing has enabled her to see the broader picture created by the pandemic. She has seen that the pathway for anyone looking to survive and thrive in their career must involve a clever combination of personal branding and candidate marketing.

Fleur's qualifications and accreditations:

- Bachelor of Economics (UWA)
- Master of Marketing (UNSW)
- Master of Tertiary Education Management (Melb.)
- Graduate Certificate in Management (UNDA)
- Qualified Careers Coach Level Two (Holistic Coach Academy)
- Fellow of the Australian Marketing Institute
- Certified Practising Marketer

Kym Kraljevic

Kym proudly calls herself a 'high-level generalist' who focuses on cultivating strong stakeholder relationships and building dynamic outcomes-focused projects and events. She seeks to work with like-minded people who also love to bring creativity and a growth mindset to build out ideas and bring them to life.

Kym has worked in government and private enterprise, and had a successful career in higher education, where she set up a student entrepreneurship training program. Other projects have included conceptualising and orchestrating events for Sydney Start-up Week, such as the Big Red London double-decker bus tours of the Sydney ecosystem and walking tours of innovation districts. She partnered with an iconic female founders' program to support female entrepreneurship, studied innovation districts to apply these frameworks to the Sydney start-up ecosystem and undertook fundraising, gained sponsorships and executed major project management.

Kym seeks diverse and challenging environments and she has turned her hand to economic policy for government, acting in Australian and international films, tv and commercials, coordinating equestrian events around the country, learning to code in Mexico, merchandising for high-end retailers and helping to set up an e-commerce platform for a major charity, as well as running her own consultancy and online businesses.

Kym's understanding of what makes businesses work, across so many industries, enables her to drill down to the essentials of starting a business. She is passionate about helping aspiring entrepreneurs to get a business idea off the ground and has a deep understanding of business planning principles and innovation frameworks.

Kym's qualifications and accreditations

- Bachelor of Arts (Advanced Major in Psychology)
- Graduate Certificate in Forensic Psychology (expected completion December 2020)

ACKNOWLEDGEMENTS

It's taken a whole throng of good folk to bring this book to fruition, especially given the tight turn-around time required to keep things relevant and current.

When I think about this book-writing journey, it's really a lifetime of experiences and learning that have made it possible. I think of my father reading to my brother and me every night of our early childhood and my mother instilling in me the confidence that I could become whatever I wanted to be.

Some of the most influential people along the way probably have no idea of the impression they left on me. There were inspirational primary school teachers, John ver Beek and Anna Ward, who always encouraged my writing, and high school English literature teacher, Roland Leach, who taught me to love words and showed me the world that literature opened up to us all. Wendy Were, a dear childhood friend, challenged me to think of creative pursuits as vital to a full human existence.

To my friends who always seemed to enjoy my university newsletters and missives from my years in Japan, thank you for building my confidence to write for an audience, as well as all the words of encouragement (and pre-release book purchases) along the way. Jane, Jo, Elspeth and Sasha deserve a special mention.

Several inspirational women played a role in me discovering my love of helping people with their career and life choices. Thank you to Prof Jennifer Nicol, who convinced the interview panel to hire me for my first job advising prospective university students on their course and career choices. I'm also very grateful to Prof Shirley Alexander, whose incredible work preparing university students for the future world of work inspired me to see higher education, job preparedness and career advice in a much broader and richer way.

A last-minute decision to attend the launch of Dr Jim Chalmers MP and Mike Quigley's 2017 book, *Changing Jobs*, (and my subsequent reading of the book) also strengthened my resolve to play some role in preparing Australians for the future world of work.

Every year since living in India in 2012 I set myself a goal of writing a book, with no result. In February 2020 I attended a workshop about writing a non-fiction book, hosted by Natasa and Stuart Denman. It was something I planned to do on the side in 2020 and the topic I was considering had nothing to do with COVID.

And the following month, as you know, I lost my full-time job, and the Career after COVID-19 podcast was launched. Thank you to my podcast co-host and contributing author for this book, Kym Kraljevic, for being impulsive and bold (like me!) and being up for the fast-paced journey into broadcasting and publishing. As I often say, Kym has one of my favourite brains in the world, and without her intellect and good humour to bounce my ideas off, and her caring sense of realism to console me in my dark moments of unemployment, Career after COVID-19 would not have got off the ground.

221

Another awesome brain and heart belong to the love of my life, Wayne, who has been endlessly patient and always encouraging as I've navigated the new world of the pandemic and how I fit within it. Thank you, my darling, for always providing the balance of security and freedom that sustains me. Not to mention supporting me to follow my dream to launch a podcast, write a book and not get sucked back into the world of full-time corporate slog, at least not yet!

I'm also so grateful to my daughter, Sayuri and son, Francis, who have shown maturity beyond their tender years in coming to terms with the pandemic and the fact that their mother has been busier and less available than usual while writing this book.

Since that February workshop, and after a few months of podcasting, and with the support of my family, I stretched to fulfil my long-held dream of writing a book. This book would not have come to be without the drive, expertise and experience of the team at Ultimate World Publishing. Natasa and Stuart, thank you for showing me that it could be done, for cheering me along, giving me ideas and encouragement. A warm thank you to my ever-patient publications coordinator, Vivienne Mason, to my editor, Marinda Wilkinson for her attention to detail and advice, and to Nikola Boskovski for his clever work laying out my cover.

Thank you to the other people who helped the book come to fruition, including careers consultant Caroline Ryan and recruiter Bill Boorman for their edits and contributions. Thanks also to a new twitter friend, Rowan Sweeney, who works in the social sector and helped me to understand the predicament of the most vulnerable in our community during the pandemic.

We have undertaken to donate ten per cent of our royalties to Beyond Blue, an Australian mental health support organisation and charity, as our way of assisting those in urgent need of mental health care.

Stay safe and well, and thank you for reading our book.

Fleur Edwards and Kym Kraljevic
Fremantle, WA and Dayboro, QLD
November 2020

223

BONUS CONTENT

As a reader of this book, you have free access to all of the resources listed throughout, without having to provide an email address or sign up to a newsletter. These include the following, as well as many others:

- Post-layoff 28-day planning tool to reduce overwhelm
- Mindset matters: Kick-starting your optimism and becoming bulletproof in 7 steps
- Who is in the mirror? The top 5 personality tests for rapid self-discovery
- Find your purpose and do what you love – a personal mission and values worksheet
- Multiply your time – 12 ways to get your life in shape
- Think outside-the-box – top 21 side hustles and niches in 2021

- Solving the entrepreneurial dilemma – a quiz to determine your suitability for self-employment
- 10-day LinkedIn profile challenge – sign up for the waitlist for the next available challenge

Visit careeraftercovid.com/boughtthebook to download any or all of these vital career and self-development tools.

Weekly inspiration

Sign up to the Career after COVID-19 email newsletter to receive weekly tips and inspiration for your career journey. Visit careeraftercovid.com/emailsignup to enter your details (we promise to keep your details safe and not to spam you!).

The Career Rockstars Facebook and LinkedIn groups are another source of inspiration and community – a place to share your journey and hear from others in a similar situation. Join the groups at:

- Facebook.com/groups/careerrockstars
- LinkedIn.com/groups/careerrockstars

TRANSFORM YOUR CAREER

WITH PERSONALISED RESOURCES AND TRAINING

The Career after COVID-19 team have developed a range of training packages to provide further, more detailed support for your career journey. The options include:

Workshops and training programs

Fleur and Kym have more than 20 years of combined experience in education, learning and development and have both received 5-star feedback for the workshops they have delivered over these decades.

We are able to present via video link or, subject to negotiation, in person to school and university groups, community organisations and commercial workplaces. Options include:

- The Future of Work
- Positive mindset for workplace success
- Next-frontier business planning and strategy

For a full list of available workshops, please visit Careeraftercovid.com/workshops

One-on-one coaching packages

These unique career and business coaching services deliver reliable insights into your personality traits, interests and suitability for various roles. The ultimate goal is to enable you to build a career that makes the most of your unique experiences and gifts.

The coaching packages are fully customisable, based on clients' needs. Options for one-on-one coaching include:

- Overshoot your potential by discovering your unfair advantage
- Standing out in the post-COVID job-hunting market

For a full list of available coaching packages, please visit Careeraftercovid.com/coaching